The da Fiore Cookbook

The da Fiore Cookbook

Recipes from Venice's Best Restaurant

Damiano Martin

with **Dana Bowen**

WILLIAM MORROW

An Imprint of HarperCollinsPublishers

HarperCollins books may be purchased for educational, business, or sales promotional use. For information please write: Special Markets Department, HarperCollins Publishers Inc., 10 East 53rd Street, New York, NY 10022.

FIRST EDITION

Designed by Leah Carlson-Stanisic

Food photography by Leonardo Frusteri

Photographs on pages 125, 137, 153, 243, and 248 courtesy Pippa Calland

Map illustration by Rodica Prato

Printed on acid-free paper

Library of Congress Cataloging-in-Publication Data has been applied for.

ISBN 0-06-009071-5

03 04 05 06 07 WBC/TP 10 9 8 7 6 5 4 3 2 1

THIS BOOK IS A DREAM THAT TOOK AWHILE TO BECOME A REALITY.

I BECAME THE MAN I AM
WITH LOVE, PASSION, AND INTROSPECTION THROUGH SHARING ALL OF LIFE'S
PRECIOUS MOMENTS WITH THOSE AROUND ME.
I DEDICATE THIS BOOK TO THE TWO PEOPLE WHO TAUGHT ME THE
TRUE TASTES AND FLAVORS OF LIFE.

Thank you **MOTHER** AND *thank you* **FATHER**.

Contents

Acknowledgments

THE IDEA FOR THE DA FIORE COOKBOOK GREW OUT OF MY DESIRE TO HONOR MY DEAR PARENTS, MARA AND MAURIZIO MARTIN, THE MOST loving, dedicated, supportive, and talented people I know. They are my greatest source of inspiration, and I thank them for embracing the idea of this book so that they may inspire others as they have always inspired me.

My thanks to journalist Marta Moretti, a longtime friend of mine and of da Fiore for creating the initial concept for the book.

Special thanks to writer Dana Bowen, who spent many months working closely with me and my family on the manuscript, and to Laura Pensiero for her tireless testing of each recipe. This book would not exist without Dana and Laura.

My deepest gratitude to BJ Carter, who guided me every step of the way. Thank you for your vision and friendship.

My appreciation goes to my agent, Michael V. Carlisle, for his support and guidance, and to photographer Leonardo Frusteri for his innovative style that brings my mother's food to life. I'd like to thank Victor Hazan for contributing kind words about my parents in the appreciation to this book. Many thanks to my editor, Harriet Bell, and her talented editorial staff at William Morrow Cookbooks, for consistently bringing style and grace to the writing and look of this book.

I'd like to thank my friends who have accompanied and helped me during this happy process, namely Mino Gasparro, Giancarlo Donativi, Alberto Quasso, and Chiara Barbisan. My thanks also to Francesco Antonucci, Nobu Matsuhisa, Danny Meyer, Paolo Veronese, Philippe Bernard, Allen and Francesca Trafficante, Serge Hajolian, Antonio and Christopher. Also, many thanks to Venini Glass.

Enormous thanks to the staff at da Fiore, especially Bruno Sissa, who is always at my mother's side in the kitchen, and to our loyal customers from Venice and all over the world. Thank you all!

by VICTOR HAZAN

THERE ARE NOT MANY RESTAURANT MEALS WHOSE TASTE CAN BE RECOL-
LECTED AND SAVORED TWENTY OR MORE YEARS AFTER THE EVENT. ONE
such exception is the supper that my wife, Marcella, and I had at da Fiore in Venice late one evening sometime between the end of the 1970s and the first year or two of the following decade. We have never got the point of dining early. Dinner for us is what wraps up the day, and as far as we are concerned no day is ready for wrapping up too long before the evening hour has struck ten times. On the evening in question we set off, hoping to dine at a quiet trattoria in the Santa Croce district of Venice run by an elderly couple much admired by the locals for the freshness and simplicity of their seafood cuisine. As we stepped inside, our eye on an empty table, the husband stopped us, explaining that we were too late, they had no fish left that night to cook. "But," he said, "there is a very young couple who have a restaurant not too far from the Rialto fish market. They stay open late and the wife is a marvelous cook."

We followed his directions and a while later a handsome man in his early twenties, who introduced

MARA *and the* **STAFF**

himself as Maurizio, the owner, showed us to a table in a room off whose low ceiling the emphatic sounds of Venetian table talk ricocheted smartly. That the dishes Maurizio brought to our table have a fond and permanent place in our memory cannot be explained just by the rarity of the ingredients. The procession of fish and shellfish may well have been encyclopedic in its variety, but we were already well acquainted with the treasures of Venice's sea. Nor were the preparations, of themselves, other than classic. What was novel and unforgettable was something ineffable that might perhaps be described as the invisibility of the cooking, the cook's ability to let the ingredients speak for themselves, eliciting from them the purest, clearest, brightest flavor that they were capable of expressing. The cook was Maurizio's wife, Mara, then just out of her teens.

The occasions thereafter on which we have had Mara's cooking are beyond counting. During the fifteen years that Marcella and I had a cooking school in Venice we welcomed the students of each course with a banquet at da Fiore. We have eaten at da Fiore with family and friends, and with colleagues. Sweetest luxury of all have been the times when my wife and I could savor Mara's wizardry at a table for two.

The story of Maurizio and Mara's success has elements of wild improbability. That two raw young farm kids with not an hour's professional experience in food could borrow money to buy a grimy old wine bar in a city as cosmopolitan and forbiddingly competitive as Venice and transform it over time into one of the world's most sought after gastronomic destinations would appear as credible as the fable of Snow White. Credit must go to Maurizio's dauntlessness, to his charm, to his winning sincerity, to his innate sense of style. Credit goes to Mara the indefatigable, Mara the phenomenal natural cook. And credit must ultimately be given to the societal values on which two youngsters were suckled, values that are appropriately inextricable from a cuisine that prizes taste over novelty and practices fidelity toward ingredients, a cuisine whose only schooling springs from that ancestral cooking academy, the family kitchen.

Carissima Mara, carissimo Maurizio:
Marcella and I raise our glasses to what you have achieved and to what,
since you are both so amazingly young still,
you may yet accomplish.

A Quick Tour of Venice

*V*ENICE IS A COLLECTION of tiny villages, or neighborhoods, each with its own personality. The main island, a fish-shaped maze of more than a hundred islets connected by footbridges and traversed by the elegant, inverted S-shaped Grand Canal, comprises six such sestiere. San Marco, with its dense concentration of historic sights and gondoliers for hire, is the best known. Despite the crowds, the sprawling Piazza San Marco, with the glittering mosaics on Basilica San Marco's façade, is one of the world's most magical places. Castello, a quieter residential neighborhood northeast of San Marco, is home to the Arsenale, the city's former shipyards that now hosts the Biennele, an international art show. The Accademia Bridge leads across the Grand Canal to Dorsoduro, where you'll find the Accademia Museum and the late Peggy Guggenheim's collection of modern art. The train station is located in Cannaregio, Venice's northernmost sestiere: Lista di Spagna, a loud avenue of modest hotels and souvenir shops leads into Strada Nova, which is packed with comfortable osterie and fashionable new bacari. The Scalzi Bridge in front of the train station crosses over to Santa Croce, a quiet area except for its Piazzale Roma, the only departure and arrival point for buses and cars. South of Santa Croce and north of Dorsoduro, connected to San Marco by the stone Rialto Bridge, sits San Polo, home to the old Rialto market and some of the city's oldest bacari and specialty food stores. This is where you find da Fiore.

Thirty miles long, and just nine miles wide, the Venetian lagoon is home to islands large and small connected by ferry. Tiny Burano is a quiet fishing village renowned for its brightly painted houses and its centuries-old tradition of Venetian lacemaking. Neighboring Murano has been the base for Venice's glass-making industry since the late thirteenth century, and visitors frequent the shops and furnaces to witness artisans at work. Giudecca, the long island across from San Marco, is home to Il Redentore, Palladio's 1577 Franciscan church. Venice Lido, a long stretch of sand that protects our part of the lagoon from the Adriatic, is the closest beach to Venice.

The islands with the greatest gastronomic significance are Torcello and Sant' Erasmo. Though Torcello played a significant role in the rise of the Venetian Republic, today only a few families remain, tending to its small farms and orchards. Sant' Erasmo is the lagoon's largest market island with sprawling fields of artichokes and fruit trees. The farmers who work the lagoon islands are faced with daunting conditions—high-rising tides and the *brezza marina,* or sea breeze, can be very cold in the winter, and abrupt climatic changes out at sea can instantly wreak havoc on crops. On the upside, the sandy soil is rich in minerals and plants of all kinds thrive here. As a result of these combined conditions, these local vegetables have their own *sapore* (taste) that's subtly salty and earthy.

Veneto

Italy

Belluno

Treviso

Vicenza

Verona

Padova

Venezia

Rovigo

• Train Station

OSTERIA
DA
FIORE

• Campo San Polo

The Grand Canal

The Grand Canal

• Saint Mark's Plaza

Welcome to da Fiore

HIDDEN AWAY ON CALLE DEL SCALETER, A QUIET VENETIAN STREET THAT CURVES OVER CANALS AND UNDER BRICK ARCHWAYS, JUST A FEW minutes' walk from the historic Rialto market on the Grand Canal, you'll find our family restaurant, da Fiore.

In many respects, da Fiore is still the same charming neighborhood osteria that my parents restored in Venice's San Polo district twenty-five years ago. Every evening, regulars meet at *Fiore,* "the flower," to chat over glasses of Prosecco in our front bar and wind down after a long day. When the lights dim at seven P.M., a familiar warmth washes over the small, wood-trimmed dining room. After the waiters finish setting the tables, my father checks each place setting. My mother enters the room, tying on her crisp, white apron and we all stop and listen as she describes the evening's menu.

In other ways, da Fiore has changed over the years. As word spread about the superb cooking and refined service at Maurizio and Mara Martin's extraordinary seafood restaurant, da Fiore became an important destination for food and fish lovers visiting Venice. When the prestigious Michelin Guide awarded da Fiore a star, my parents knew that their hard work had placed our family restaurant on the world's culinary map.

I was introduced to the pleasures of the Venetian table at an early age, having grown up in my father's elegant dining room and my mother's bustling kitchen. Mara and Maurizio have great respect for the city's culinary spirit, and they instilled in me a deep appreciation for the spirit behind da Fiore's daily-changing menu. More than an appetite, this spirit is an insatiable approach to life characterized by uniquely Venetian impulses: to enjoy a midday glass of wine with a friend, for example, or to sprinkle a little spice into the pot and create something beautiful on the plate. It's the charm of this city, compounded by constant reflection in these shimmering canals that has a way of heightening our senses: music sounds clearer, light glows more brilliantly, and flavors taste brighter in Venice.

My parents channel this spirit into da Fiore every night. In traditional Venetian fashion, Mara cooks seasonal fish and vegetables simply and delicately, without heavy sauces that would mask their fresh flavor. But she doesn't shy away from innovation, and so da Fiore's food appeals to modern tastes. Few of her recipes contain more than a handful of ingredients, and most take less than a half hour to prepare, yet they are sophisticated in their simplicity. Her famous fillet of sole, wrapped around zucchini matchsticks and a pair of basil leaves, anointed with a few glistening drops of young Ligurian olive oil, is a perfect example. Cooked for mere minutes, it tastes of summer on a plate.

da Fiore's Early Days

On the morning of April 1, 1978, Mara fired up the grill in her new kitchen and started cooking. When the homey aromas of herb-laden fish and grilled polenta lured curious passersby inside, Maurizio greeted them with a warm welcome and a glass of wine. Osteria da Fiore was officially open for business.

The da Fiore story begins much earlier, in the verdant countryside that sprawls across the Veneto in a blanket of green fields and farms. My parents were born in the small town of Mirano, just fifteen miles north of Venice. Mara and Maurizio have known one another for as long as either one of them can remember, having grown up just a mile apart in their tightly knit, agricultural community. After these high school sweethearts were married, they jumped at an offer to work for an aunt who owned an osteria in Treviso.

The prospect of working together immediately struck a chord, and though neither one had restaurant experience, they were eager to give it a go. My father tended to the front of the house with pleasure, and the kitchen beckoned to my mother's quiet creativity. Mara had never studied cooking, but she intuitively knew her way around a kitchen. Her grandmother was a chef in Mirano whom locals recruited to cater weddings and other celebrations, and Mara was her self-appointed assistant. Her feasts were legendary and, when we visit Mirano, people still recollect and rave about them.

One winter day, Mara's father came home from work in Venice and told my parents about a restaurant where he and his co-workers had been having lunch lately. Da Fiore was a time-worn bacaro, the kind of place where locals stopped in for quick, casual meals and old men played cards on lazy afternoons—and it was for sale.

In the late seventies, Venice was just as tourist-driven as it is today. But the early movements to "Save Venice" were in the works, and many young people were moving back to the city and pouring their creative energies into restoring buildings and businesses that catered to the local community. Mara and Maurizio decided to make the leap, and this affable spot in San Polo's lively residential district was just the place.

They spent months renovating. When it came to designing the menu, they realized that they were in new territory—*fish* territory. In Mirano, fish rarely found its way onto the menu—country fare such as meat and game birds were the main dishes of choice. Mara approached the subject with serious curiosity. She sought the help of an elderly cook named Vittorio, a walking encyclopedia on Venetian fish who came to da Fiore each morning after Mara returned from the market and showed her how to clean and cook the local specialties. Gradually, her sea legs got stronger, and with them she discovered a subject that was ceaselessly fascinating and adaptable.

At first, Mara lined the bar with a simple menu of colorful cicheti, Venice's traditional bar snacks: platters of *sarde in saor,* sweet and sour fried sardines in an onion and raisin marinade; oven-roasted scallops on the half shell; and creamy codfish puree. Regulars soon convinced Mara and Maurizio to offer sit-down, multicourse dinners. Mara's early meals were simple and traditional: risottos or soups followed by whole grilled fish and local vegetables and finished with a classic dessert. Maurizio filled the front window every morning with an eye-catching array of fresh fish to alert the crowds that da Fiore had graduated from a *bacaro* to an *osteria.*

By word of mouth, news of an osteria that served perfectly cooked seafood in San Polo spread all over town, and da Fiore was soon packed nightly. Mara began experimenting more in the kitchen, and her guests eagerly embraced these early innovations. Instead of serving traditional grilled whole fish with vegetables on the side, she prepared fillets and integrated vegetables and fruit into her recipes for color, texture, and flavor.

Before long, Mara's cooking was known throughout Venice. In the early eighties, my parents turned their attention to the look of the restaurant, whose old-fashioned sensibility belied the new culinary territory they were charting. They put in air conditioning. They draped the tables with linen and ordered new plates and glasses. Da Fiore gradually transformed into an elegant trattoria.

It was the beginning of a new era for da Fiore. Our reservation book was filled every night, film stars and politicians, artists and musicians were quietly recognized, and more international guests were tracking us down.

There was never a question that I would learn every aspect of our family business. For years, I watched and learned from my mother in her kitchen. When I was barely knee-high, she'd put my tiny, fingers to the delicate task of peeling *schie*, the small brown shrimp from the lagoon. I was promoted to *lavapiatti*—dishwasher, a role I was happy to relinquish when my father asked me if I'd like to help him in the dining room.

Today, da Fiore is the epitome of elegance. There's a private nook flanked by plush banquettes where groups can dine in privacy. Warm, autumnal colors wrap the dining room—the walls are draped in silk, the silver sparkles, and the linen is crisp. There is a single table on the *terrazza* overlooking the canal, impervious to formal flourishes, reserved for a romantic couple. And when old friends return for a meal, they know that Mara has something special for them in the kitchen, and that Maurizio will greet them at the door with a warm welcome and a glass of wine.

da Fiore's Venetian Cuisine

It wasn't until I came to work in New York that I realized how few Americans had crossed paths with Venice's true culinary spirit. I shuddered to hear people describe their Venetian dining experiences: more often than not, at another turnkey restaurant near Piazza San Marco serving yet another uninspired meal. These tired rotations of "authentic" recipes, prepared day in and day out regardless of the season, are unfortunate consequences of Venice's vibrant tourist trade. Worst of all, they send visitors home with the impression that our cuisine hasn't had a good idea since the days of the doges, which couldn't be farther from the truth.

As any traveler willing to stray from the tourist path will discover, Venetian cooking is alive, well, and always evolving. We have famously adventurous taste buds: when the East met the West at the Rialto market five hundred years ago, Venice became Europe's epicenter of trade and its first full-fledged culinary melting pot. Early Venetian cooks approached exotic ingredients from distant tables with a curious, daring artistry that continues to distinguish our local cuisine.

There have always been two sides to Venetian cuisine: the elaborate, spice-laden feasts hosted by the doges and noble families, and the hearty, practical fishermen's meals prepared at home. These traditions eventually met in the middle and gave rise to one cuisine that is both humble and ambitious, rustic and refined, earthy and exquisite.

La cucina Veneziana has always been inspired by the countryside that surrounds it. The Veneto is one of the most geographically diverse and agriculturally affluent regions in Italy, and it has been nourishing urban appetites by exporting staples such as polenta and rice, flour and wine into the city's markets for centuries. This exchange is reciprocal: when Mara is cooking in the country, she looks to the region's capital for access to international ingredients. As a result, Venice and the towns of the Veneto—among them Padova and Verona, Vicenza and Treviso—share many culinary common denominators, although they each offer regional specialties of their own.

From the rich coastal lowlands, west across the fertile plains of the Po Valley known as the *pianura Padana,* and north to the rocky Dolomites that lead into the snow-capped Alps, the Veneto comprises what was once the most powerful region of the Venetian Republic. The Po River to the south; the Adige just above; the Piave and the Tagliamento to the north wind through this region, irrigating miles and miles of rice flats and cornfields, which explains why rice and polenta are the starches of choice. Dairy farms outnumber olive groves inland, and as a result butter is used more often than olive oil in traditional kitchens. Orchards, vegetable crops, and vineyards flourish here.

The Veneto's neighboring regions fell under the Venetian Republic's sphere of influence and continue to exchange culinary traditions with the capital city today. Trentino–Alto Adige, which is also called Süd Tirol, borders Switzerland and Austria to the northwest. From speck (smoked, cured ham) to strudel, its Austrian-influenced ingredients find their way onto da Fiore's menu. On the northern edge of the Gulf of Venezia, bordering Slovenia to the east, sits Friuli–Venezia Giulia, where rustic specialties such as frico (fried Montasio cheese) and roasted meats prevail. Along the coast, in Trieste and on islands such as Grado and Istria, seafood is the star.

Mara also dips into cuisines that helped shape Venetian cooking, employing the Eastern influences of sweet-sour marinades with one hand, and drawing on the familiar, earthy flavors of her native Veneto countryside with the other. She embraces traditional recipes, as well as inspirations of her own. More than any other influence, the seasons inform her meals: she's been called an architect of flavor for her intuitive ability to build masterpieces from local fish and vegetables at their peak.

News of da Fiore and Mara's Venetian cooking has traveled *da boca a boca*—by word of mouth—among food lovers in Venice and beyond. We've been flattered to have our recipes featured in international cookbooks, and journalists from American and European culinary magazines have traveled to Venice to learn my parents' secrets and observe their methods.

As I always tell our guests, there are no secrets. Da Fiore's success over the years stems from my parents' love of Venetian cooking and their respect for the way it brings people together around the table. Toward the end of dinner service, when the pace of the restaurant slows down, I often catch them sharing this joy with others: my father, pouring a taste of fine grappa for a curious guest; my mother, jotting down a recipe on the back of a menu for someone to take home.

Our guests often ask for a memento of their visit, a keepsake to recall the fleeting flavors when they return home. A cookbook, perhaps, so they could replicate these meals in their own kitchen? I've always hoped that my parents would someday behold such a collection—the sum of their life's work and shared careers. And so, this cookbook is as much a gift for them as it is for our cherished guests. I've collected these time-honored, signature da Fiore recipes, with my mother's cooking wisdom and my father's wine suggestions. Whether you've been to Venice countless times or intend to visit someday, my hope is that *The da Fiore Cookbook* helps bring our inimitable Venetian culinary spirit into your own kitchen to share and enjoy with family and friends.

The Seasons of the Rialto Market

It's seven A.M. and Mara and Maurizio are standing at the intersection of Campo de la Pescheria and the Grand Canal, in the heart of the Rialto market. The scene is a frenzy of activity. Merchants carry colorful crates from wooden boats that rock alongside the moorings, while shoppers angle for their share of the freshest fish, fruit, and vegetables from the Venetian lagoon and mainland farms.

The seasonal sway of Venice's collective cravings—for softshell crabs in spring, radicchio in the fall, and tiny, sweet shrimp when the waters are cold, for example—is most apparent here, in the bustling market stalls near the Rialto Bridge. The air is heavy with the sweet smell of live fish and the deep, warm earthiness of just-picked vegetables. Fishmongering, Venetian-style, is already in full swing under the tall porticos of La Pescheria, the fish market.

This is where our meals begin at da Fiore. Like all Italian cooks, Mara is most attracted to the little white signs upon which are scribbled NOSTRANO. Translated as "our"—as in "our artichokes" or "our squid"—the term assures us that these ingredients hail from our local farms and waters. Mara's heart skips a beat when she finally sees the sign CORNETTI NOSTRANI sticking out of a crate. You can be sure that these tiny purple beans will be on that night's menu.

Even in the venerable Rialto market, seasonality has become less apparent over the past decade. Although one can find a juicy peach in the winter these days, flown in from some faraway place, as a rule Venetian cooks like my mother would rather wait until summer, when we can enjoy our own.

The Rialto dates back to the thirteenth century and is the oldest market in Venice. For home shoppers, it's the market of choice for produce and seafood. What we don't grow in our country garden, we buy here, but fish is another story: the infrastructure of the Venetian market system is more complicated than the friendly Rialto suggests. Many of the ingredients sold at the Rialto were purchased from the larger Chioggia market twenty-five miles to the south, which serves as a commercial hub for markets all across the country. For the restaurant, we buy our fish at the Mercato all' Ingrosso in Tronchetto, where fish and shellfish come straight off the fishing boats. Andrea, da Fiore's fish buyer, unhitches our wooden, flat-bottomed boat from da Fiore's landing and takes it out to Tronchetto before dawn. He often calls Mara from his cell phone to describe the day's catch, and when he returns with her order, Maurizio helps him unload the fish, checking each specimen before passing it on to the kitchen staff to prepare for cooking.

All markets are closed on Sundays and Mondays, and that's why da Fiore is closed on those days as well.

The Rialto market is located in San Polo, close to the Rialto Bridge, and just above the Grand Canal's sharpest bend. You can walk there or take the vaporetto to the Rialto stop. The easiest and most majestic approach to the market is by traghetti that depart from Ca d'Oro in Canareggio and drop you off at the banks of the market.

The Flavors of Venice

Venice is a city built on elaborate artifice, with gregarious gondoliers, proud palazzi, and picture-perfect canals, yet it rarely reveals its true character to the 14 million people who visit each year. Behind these facades, the real Venice enjoys a hidden life of its own, with social rhythms and culinary cravings particular to its locals.

Venice is home to just 60,000 people today, while the mainland suburb of Mestre on *terra ferma* has swelled to more than 250,000. Every morning thousands of suburbanites drive to work over the long causeway from Mestre to Venice, giving the impression of the city having a much larger population. True Venetians are immediately recognized by their dialect: its melodic cadence is softened by the complete absence of l's and d's. You'll notice this on some menus, where *brodetto* becomes *broeto,* and *bigoli* is *bigoi*. While some words are similar to Italian, Venetian is a different language entirely, with Spanish, French, Greek, and Arabic reminders of the cross-cultural conversations exchanged during the days of the spice trade.

Venice is smaller than many people imagine: you could walk from one end to the other in less than an hour, if you're not distracted. But who's not distracted? We can hardly leave the house without seeing someone we know, and when we do, we catch up over a quick glass of wine and a bite to eat at the closest *osteria*. After you've said your good-byes and are on your way, you spot someone else, and the cycle begins again. Over time, these friendly habits gave rise to *cicheti* and *ombre,* a miniature menu designed to accompany these frequent, impromptu get-togethers.

Cicheti are small servings of simply prepared foods that Venetians devour from morning to midnight. Similar to Spanish tapas and Greek meze, they're available at nearly every bacaro and osteria. A rustic back-street bacaro may display a few traditional cicheti, like fried sardines and marinated octopus, while trendier osterie turn their colorful, cicheti-lined bars into meeting places. The protocol remains the same: you select your snack by pointing, and usually eat it standing up. Each one costs just a Euro or two.

Accompanying cicheti is the ombra, a tiny glass of wine that holds no more than a few sips. *Ombra* refers to the shadow that the Campanile in Piazza San Marco created. Wine merchants of the now long-gone market were always chasing the shadow to keep their wines cool, and shoppers would follow to sip wine in the shade.

There used to be hundreds of casual bacari and osterie around town, with clunky wood tables and oversize barrels dispensing local wines. In fact, da Fiore began life as one, long before my parents took over. But when tourism became Venice's chief business, many shut down. About twenty-five years ago, young people like my parents started reopening these bacari and recultivating the tradition.

Today, Venice is cicheti obsessed. In other Italian towns, people *fare una passegiata* (take a stroll) before dinner, while Venetians *fare un giro di ombre* (tour around for ombre), stopping at several bacari and osterie over the course of an evening.

da Fiore's Country Garden

As the days grow warmer and the landscape shows the first hint of green after a long, dark winter, we're anxious to see what's stirring in our country garden. For generations, our family has tended this *orto,* or vegetable garden, behind our house in Mirano. When we're working in Venice, Maurizio's father keeps watch over these two large parcels of land lined with pomegranate and apricot trees. In the summer, we pass long evenings with friends outside at a table canopied by a large kiwi tree, and country roasts are prepared in the outdoor wood-burning oven. When it's time to head back to the city, bags and basketsful of tomatoes and zucchini, fennel and eggplants, fresh and wild herbs, return with us to da Fiore's kitchen.

It's in country gardens like these that we embrace the ancient flavors of *erbe aromatiche e selvatiche*—aromatic and wild herbs. Aromatics such as basil, rosemary, sage, mint, marjoram, and thyme are the best known. The wild herbs, *erbette di campo,* add an element of seasonal surprise, since they can't be cultivated for commercial sale. There's a river near our house and, come springtime, you can find every wild herb imaginable lining its banks. *Ortiche,* or wild nettles, give off an earthy flavor once their stingers settle when cooked. They become a bright green base for one of da Fiore's favorite soups. Wild fennel and wild radicchio display the rustic alter egos of their tamed cousins.

Mara's Fish Kitchen

The fish, shellfish, and crustaceans that crowd the Venetian lagoon and its surrounding Adriatic are the star characters in da Fiore's kitchen. We're indebted to the elements at work in the lagoon's shallow, brackish waters: sea tides wash away impurities that would otherwise settle on the lagoon floor, and freshwater streams fed by melted snow from the Alps and Dolomites keep the lagoon cool as late as March (or if we're lucky, April). These forces conspire to create a clean, thriving habitat for our fish, which are revered for their small size, sweet taste, and delicate texture.

Migratory fish swim into the lagoon at different times of the year, and local fisherman wait for them in flat-bottomed boats equipped with different nets for catching each species. Their *pesce di valle* that farm some breeds look like old, run-down fishing shacks floating on the water. Due to overfishing, there are fewer fish in Venice's lagoon than ever before, and regulations are in effect to secure the survival of certain species. When the lagoon shuts down for Fermo Pesca a few weeks each year to replenish the local fish population, we close da Fiore and go on vacation. But over the course of the year, if a few of our local species aren't available, we seek out fresh fish from elsewhere.

Seafood is a regional and seasonal subject: red mullet from the sandy Gulf of Venice tastes different from red mullet caught along the rockier Dalmatian coast, for example, and their flavors differ depending upon the time of the year. What's more, the same species of fish often goes by a different name in different places. But these variables aren't detriments. You don't have to be in Venice nor must you use Venetian fish to cook like a Venetian. In the recipes that follow, we supply substitutions and hope that you will experiment with what's fresh and local in your market.

American guests tell us that they enjoy eating fish in restaurants and appreciate the nutritional benefits, but they rarely cook it at home. Mara doesn't think that the challenge is cooking fish—that's the easy part! Instead, it's shopping for fish that many cooks struggle with. The answer is to find a reliable fishmonger who runs a clean, iced-down fish market or counter near you, and keep going back until he knows who you are. He will guide you toward the best seasonal fish available and shuck or fillet or clean anything you don't feel prepared to handle yourself.

BUYING FISH A fresh fish looks very much alive. Its eyes should look clear and bright, not cloudy, and should bulge out, not sink down. The gills should be red, not gray, and wet, not dry—if they're brown, the fish has likely been frozen. Look for firm flesh that's glossy and not a bit slimy: it should bounce back when you lightly press it. Fish should smell of the sea, but never "fishy." Ask to smell it. The skin and scales should be shiny, and the fins should be flexible. Fillets should be firm with no red streaks or brown edges, which are signs of age. Never buy fish that is wrapped in plastic.

In Venice, we prefer small fish for their delicate, tender, and sweeter flesh. Whenever you can, select a smaller specimen over a larger one. As a general rule, plan on a third to a half pound of fillets per person, and a pound of whole fish per person.

STORING FISH In a perfect world, we wouldn't buy fish until moments before cooking it. But let's be realistic, it's fine to refrigerate fish in a plastic bag for an hour. If your purchase needs to wait for a few hours, however, here's what we suggest. Fillets and whole fish should be kept wrapped in parchment or butcher's paper on ice in the refrigerator (never directly on the ice)—we use a sheet pan with holes on the bottom so that the melting ice water can drain. Storing bivalves in a bowl in the refrigerator is adequate, but we prefer to wrap them tightly first in a moist, oversized kitchen towel. Never store them on ice. Live crustaceans, such as lobsters, should be held in a covered colander so that they can breathe.

FROZEN FISH Although we never buy frozen fish at da Fiore, we do know that most frozen fish nowadays is flash frozen and yields terrific results. When purchasing frozen fish, make sure there are no signs of white freezer burn. Allow fish to thaw slowly in the refrigerator. Use it immediately and do not freeze it again. Fish that's been previously frozen and is sold as fresh has a soft, almost mushy texture.

CLEANING AND SCALING FISH Ask your fishmonger to clean and scale your fish—most will expect to. If you opt to do it yourself, wet the fish and, holding the head down with one hand, use the other hand to scrape from the tail up toward the head with either the back of a knife or a fish scaler.

FILLETING FISH Mara uses a Japanese sushi-style knife with a thin, flexible blade for filleting flatfish, and a sturdier fillet knife for round fish. For round fish, begin by making an incision along the bottom of the fish from under the head to the tail, and remove the innards. For flatfish, once you make an incision to remove the head, the innards can easily be pulled out. If you're cooking a whole fish remove the gills and fins: It's easy to do—just cut away the gills under the flap on the cheeks with your knife or kitchen shears, and snip off the fins with scissors.

Flat-bodied fish such as sole, halibut, flounder, and turbot have both eyes on one side and a spine that goes through the center, with four small fillets, two on each side. In Venice, many of our flatfish are so small that they have only two fillets, one on either side. Place the fish eye-side up and slice a V just behind the head. With kitchen shears, snip away the fins that line the top and bottom of the fish to facilitate easy removal of the skin. Holding the head down with one hand, gently insert the blade of your knife between the skin and meat. Once you've pulled away enough skin with your knife to grip it with your hand, pull it up and away from the head until it's completely detached from the meat all the way down to the tail. Then, starting from the head and working down, slice through with your knife flat against the rib bones, pull away the fillet above the spine with your hands, and then pull away the one below. Turn the fish over and remove the skin and the remaining two fillets in the same fashion.

Round-bodied fish such as sea bream and bass have eyes on either side and a spine that runs near the top of the fish. Make an incision with the tip of your knife on either side of both the top fin and the bottom one—not only will this remove the fins but it will loosen the skin. Make an incision around the head and gills, and then, beginning at the tail, slide your knife between the skin and the meat. Once you've lifted up enough of the skin to get a grip on it, instead of pulling it up toward the head with your hand, wrap your knife around it and start rolling it back, away from the tail. This is easier on your arms, and it will neatly pull the skin away from the meat. Do this on both sides. Once the skin is removed, begin to fillet the first side of the body by making an incision along the backbone with a very sharp knife. Slide the blade down one side of the backbone, then along the ribs, lifting the meat as you go. Turn the fish over and remove the second fillet in the same fashion. Lay the fillets on the sides from which you removed the skin and feel down the center for small bones. Using tweezers or small pliers, pull these out.

COOKING FISH This is a delicate but flexible art. We hesitate to give precise cooking times in these recipes, since temperatures vary widely from oven to oven, stovetop to stovetop, and grill to grill. Fish doesn't take long to prepare—as soon as it turns from translucent to white and when the flesh stiffens to the touch and flakes but is still moist and yielding, it's done. Perhaps more than any other ingredient, fish requires constant testing—with your fork, your finger, your eyes, and your nose!

Venetian Basics

Here are the staple ingredients that stock our shelves at home and at da Fiore, as well as the techniques and basic recipes we rely on.

BUTTER AND OILS Butter is traditionally used more than olive oil in the Veneto, but at da Fiore both play an important role. When Mara desires a rich undertone in a pasta dish, she starts the sauce with butter. Before serving a risotto, she stirs in a bit of butter to add a rich, glossy sheen.

For frying fish and starting risotto, Mara uses sunflower oil, as olive oil tends to assert itself over mild ingredients. Sunflower oil is becoming more readily available in North American markets, but safflower oil or corn oil are good substitutes.

Fish finds no better partner than a *filo,* or a drizzled thread of fine olive oil used in moderation. We have a table full of extra virgin olive oils from all over Italy at da Fiore, and we call on different ones for different culinary purposes. For our fish antipasti, we generally use olive oil from Liguria, which has a fruity lightness that goes well with seafood. A more assertive Tuscan oil, one with a slightly bitter edge, is preferred for salads and cooked vegetables. For *secondi,* or our main fish and vegetable dishes, Mara reaches for a light Umbrian oil most often. For most pasta, a more robust, earthy Pugliese oil is preferred. At home, we simply rely on a good, mildly flavored extra virgin oil for most uses.

CITRUS JUICE AND VINEGAR Mara loves the bright lift that fresh citrus juice gives to fish, whether it's the sweet tang of orange or the bracing acidity of grapefruit. Red and white wine vinegar are the more traditional vinegars used in Venetian cooking, but we also keep a few kinds of *balsamico* on hand. *Aceto Balsamico Tradizionale di Modena*, a naturally sweet concentration that spends at least twelve years in progressively smaller barrels made out of different types of aromatic wood, adds a soft, sweet/sour flavor when drizzled over risotto or fish. The more time spent in the barrel, the more expensive the final product. We reserve a small bottle of one-hundred-year-old balsamico, which is naturally concentrated down to a thick, molasses-like syrup, for very special meals. For our fish dishes that call for a fine balsamico, a thirty-year-old specimen is perfect, and if it happens to be a bit too loose, we refrigerate it to thicken it. We use *condimento di Modena,* a younger, lighter vinegar, for dressing salads.

VENETIAN SPICES AND SEASONINGS Although we probably use various spices more than other regions in Italy, subtlety is the key to our cuisine. We use white pepper more often than black pepper, as it's less assertive and more well rounded. Mara sometimes flavors fresh pasta with saffron, but in Venice, it's considered too strong for most fish dishes. Nutmeg, cloves, and cinnamon find their way into many traditional recipes.

The salt that we use, and the one that best complements fish, is sea salt, which has a clean, fresh taste. Used toward the end of cooking, or sprinkled over a finished dish, fine-grained sea salt brightens and clarifies flavors.

Polenta, Then and Now

WHEN CORNMEAL ARRIVED in the Veneto from the New World, it was called *grano Turco,* or Turkish grain—a moniker which suggests its exotic allure rather than its actual provenance. By the mid-sixteenth century, farmers from the Veneto were growing corn and selling polenta.

Polenta was traditionally prepared in a copper kettle known as a *caliera,* which hung from a heavy chain over a fire in an open kitchen hearth. Cooks used a long wooden spoon to stir so that the bubbling, splattering porridge wouldn't burn their hands and arms. Polenta still requires constant stirring for forty minutes or more, but some cooks who make it frequently use a *salvafiamma,* a mechanical mixer that attaches to the pot and stirs the polenta. At da Fiore and at home, Mara prefers the old-fashioned method.

Basic Recipes

Though polenta is a common thread in the Veneto's regional cuisines, there's controversy over the subject of cornmeal. The coarse, full-flavored yellow polenta is most popular on the mainland, where it's often poured out onto a wooden board called a *tagliere di legno* and topped with roasted meats, sausages, or game birds. In Venice, however, the preferred polenta is fine white cornmeal made only from the white part of the corn kernels. Its refined taste and creamy texture pairs beautifully with fish.

Our kitchen would come to a halt without polenta. Mara prepares both kinds to accompany *antipasti* and *secondi*. After stirring for a full forty minutes, she pours the polenta porridge into an inch-high baking pan, lets it cool and harden, slices it into long rectangles or triangles, and broils or grills the pieces before serving them on the side. Cooked polenta is also cut into cubes and roasted in the oven, or simply spooned soft onto a plate.

If yellow or white Italian polenta is unavailable, buy coarse stone-ground cornmeal.

Polenta

Makes 4 servings

1 quart water
¾ teaspoon salt
2 tablespoons olive oil
1 cup coarse-grain cornmeal

In a heavy-bottomed medium saucepan, bring the water to a boil. Add the salt and oil. Add the polenta in a slow, steady stream, whisking constantly; the water should stay at a moderate boil. When all of the cornmeal is in the pan, cook, stirring with a wooden spoon almost constantly, for 40 minutes. The polenta should thicken and pull away from the sides of the pan as you stir. Serve while soft and hot.

This simple fish broth is the foundation of da Fiore's cuisine. It lends a backdrop of flavor to risottos and soups, coaxes fish in the pan to release its juices, and provides a sweet and slightly briny backdrop to pasta sauces.

Home cooks often shudder at the thought of making brodo, thinking that they'll have to devote an entire afternoon to the task. The fact is that Italian fish and vegetable broths are less concentrated and laborious than French stocks. Our brodo begins every morning, shortly after Maurizio has checked in the day's catch. As each cook cleans his lot, the shells, heads, and bones are tossed into a huge, boiling pot, and the broth is ready by the time we start lunch service.

This all-purpose fish broth can be frozen for a month. With the exception of strongly flavored fatty fish such as bluefish or sardines, use almost any type of fish available. You can always prepare a quick broth using whatever fish you're working with at the moment—whether it's shrimp shells or the head and bones of a single fish.

Fish Broth

Brodo di Pesce   *Makes 2 quarts*

2½ pounds bones and heads from fish such as red mullet,
    sole, monkfish, or turbot
Shells from 8 ounces peeled shrimp (optional)
2½ quarts water
2 celery stalks
¼ small onion
1 garlic clove
2 bay leaves
1 sprig thyme
4 black peppercorns

Rinse the fish bones to remove any trace of blood, which can make the stock bitter. Place all the ingredients in a pot. Bring the broth to a gentle simmer over medium heat and cook for 30 minutes, skimming the surface frequently to remove the foamy scum or impurities. If using immediately, ladle the stock from the pot into your preparation. Otherwise, strain the stock through a fine-mesh strainer into a container. Cool in an ice bath, then cover and refrigerate for up to two days.

This fragrant easy-to-prepare broth is the reason that we never think of using bouillon cubes. If you're preparing the Risotto with Aromatic Herbs (page 105), add a handful of herbs to the broth as it cooks.

Vegetable Broth

Brodo di Verdure *Makes 2 quarts*

2 celery stalks, halved
2 medium carrots, halved
1 small onion, halved
2½ quarts water

Combine all the ingredients in a pot. Bring to a boil. Reduce the heat and simmer, uncovered, for 30 minutes. Strain and discard the vegetables. Cool and refrigerate for up to 4 days.

Venice in Winter

VENICE LOOKS HER LOVELIEST in the wintertime. A dusting of snow often covers the rooftops, and the Grand Canal, shrouded in a heavy white fog one minute, is crystal-clear and luminous the next. Sure, the footbridges and campos can be dangerously slippery, and an icy lagoon can set back a city dependent on water transport, but it's a small price to pay for the rare pleasure of having the city all to yourself. Locals enjoy this seasonal lull while they can—the frenetic pace will snap back when the tourists return for Carnivale. Winter is also a perfect time for the culinary-minded traveler to pay a visit. Our local fish are at the smallest and sweetest, and after the Fermo Pesca restrictions are lifted, shellfish are at their best. Though the streets seem empty and still, the Rialto is as bustling as ever as harvests of radicchio, broccoli, winter squash, and countless other local vegetables stream in from the islands and the mainland. At da Fiore, holiday meals are long and leisurely under twinkling Christmas lights and gold garlands.

The Spice Trade's Enduring Tradition

As early as A.D. 1000, Venice was the culinary center of Europe. Merchants from the Far East, Spain, Portugal, France, and North Africa traded their goods on the Rialto Bridge, and Venice sent its merchants out to the ends of the navigable world in search of exotic new flavors. The famous bags of spices known as *sacchettis Venetis* were sold as luxury goods: black pepper, at one point, was almost as expensive as gold, and nutmeg, cinnamon, cloves, and saffron all fetched astronomical prices. When Venetian explorers such as Marco Polo and Niccola del Conti discovered the origins of these spices and revealed new routes to their sources, the city became rich from culinary commerce.

Venetians celebrated the city's wealth at the dinner table. The feasts hosted by the doges, the Republic's leaders, were famously over the top, and foreign dignitaries were treated to splendid table settings and lavish menus. Even as late as the Renaissance, spices were valued for their medicinal properties, so anyone who could afford to cook with them did so with abandon, considering their meals all the more fortifying. But most Venetians couldn't afford these precious flavorings, which explains why the dishes that have endured five hundred years after the decline of the Venetian Republic use them sparingly.

A regular accompaniment to our main courses, this flavorful rice begins on the stove and finishes in the oven. We use long-grain rice, which is lighter and less starchy than shorter-grained risotto varieties.

da Fiore Baked Rice

Riso al Forno *Makes 4 servings (about 3 cups)*

2 tablespoons unsalted butter
1 small onion, halved
3 cloves
1 bay leaf
1¼ cups long-grain rice
2½ cups Fish Broth (page 14) or water

Preheat the oven to 400°F.

Rub the bottom of a medium, ovenproof saucepan with a tablespoon of the butter. Push the cloves through the bay leaf and fix the bay leaf to the flat side of half an onion. Place both halves in the saucepan, flat side down. Cook over medium heat until fragrant and the bottom just starts to brown, about 5 minutes. Add the rice and remaining tablespoon butter. Cook, stirring, for about a minute to "toast" the rice. Add the broth, bring to a boil, then remove from the heat; cover and transfer to the oven. Cook until the rice is tender and the broth has been absorbed, about 15 minutes. Remove the pan from the oven and let the rice stand, covered, for 5 minutes. Discard the onion, cloves, and bay leaf and fluff the rice with a fork before serving.

Antipasti

As THEIR NAME SUGGESTS, THESE SAVORY BITES ARRIVE BEFORE THE MEAL TO PIQUE THE APPETITE FOR THE FEAST TO FOLLOW. OUR ANTIpasti includes many of Venice's venerable recipes, such as creamy codfish *baccalà mantecato* served with polenta squares and the marinated *sarde in saor* steeped with onions, raisins, and pine nuts. Venetian home cooks often keep these on hand to serve at the start of a meal.

Though Venetians, like all Italians, eat their vegetables as a side dish of the main course, or *secondo,* we often integrate local seasonal produce into antipasti. In early spring, a favorite is *castraure con arance e Parmigiano-Reggiano*, a salad made with baby artichokes, oranges, and slivers of Parmigiano-Reggiano. In the fall, when wild mushrooms flood the market, we thinly slice them and toss them with truffled *tomino* cheese.

Baskets full of fresh, young greens are always on hand at da Fiore to serve as a base for our antipasti salads. Each green has its own flavor, be it the peppery *rucola*, assertive *radicchio rosso,* or bittersweet *puntarelle.* Mara prefers to dress green salads with her hands, because utensils aren't as effective in coating every leaf. First toss the greens with some salt, then add the acid, whether vinegar or citrus juice. Finally, drizzle the greens with olive oil and season with pepper.

This creamy codfish recipe has been spooned onto grilled polenta in Venetian bars, restaurants, and home kitchens for centuries. Similar to France's *brandade de morue,* our *baccalà mantecato,* which means "mashed cod," is a Venetian classic.

Whipped Venetian Codfish

Baccalà Mantecato alla Veneziana *Makes 6 servings*

8 to 10 ounces dried cod (preferably *stoccafisso ragno*), or
    salt cod if unavailable
1 quart milk
3 quarts water
1 small onion, halved
1 celery stalk, halved
1 garlic clove, crushed
½ to ¾ cup extra virgin olive oil
2 tablespoons finely chopped flat-leaf parsley
Salt and freshly ground black pepper
½ head radicchio di Chioggia, cut into thin ribbons
½ head Boston lettuce, cut into thin ribbons
12 slices polenta (page 13)

Soak the cod for 4 days in a large saucepan filled with cold water, changing the water twice a day. Remove the cod from the water. Pull off any skin and, using kitchen pliers or tweezers, remove any bones from the spine.

In a medium saucepan, combine the milk and water. Add the onion, celery, and garlic, and season with salt (omit if using salt cod). Bring the mixture to a boil. Lower the heat and simmer for 20 minutes. Remove from the heat. Transfer the cod to the bowl of a standing mixer fitted with the paddle attachment. Add just enough of the cooking liquid to moisten the fish, ¼ to ½ cup; make sure that the garlic clove is not included. Beat the cod on low speed. When it breaks into small pieces, increase the mixing speed and begin adding the olive oil in a thin, steady stream. The quantity of the oil used depends on the quality and fat content of the cod; stop adding oil when the mixture is very creamy and emulsified. Stir in the parsley and season with salt, if necessary, and pepper. Using an oval ice cream scoop, neatly place three mounds of baccalà on each serving plate. Sprinkle with a handful of radicchio and Boston lettuce garnish. Serve with grilled or sautéed wedges of polenta.

There's no better showcase than this for the sweet, nutlike flavor of fresh, meaty scallops just shucked from their shells. We use scallops from the north of Venice, the same species as the fan-shaped, corrugated *Coquilles Saint-Jacques* harvested throughout the Mediterranean. Large sea scallops are a fine substitute for this recipe, although getting them in the shell may require calling your fishmonger ahead of time. Since scallops perish more quickly in their shells than other bivalves, most are shucked at sea and packaged for sale. You can buy these and purchase shells for presentation, but you'll miss the sweet red coral that adds another dimension to this dish.

Scallops in Their Shells with Thyme

Cappesante Gratinate al Timo *Makes 6 servings*

Coarse salt to line serving plates
18 fresh scallops in their shells
Salt and freshly ground black pepper
Leaves from 2 thyme sprigs
3 tablespoons finely grated Parmigiano-Reggiano
3 tablespoons finely ground fresh breadcrumbs (see page 32)
3 tablespoons olive oil

Preheat the oven to 475°F.

Line the bottoms of six serving plates with ½ inch coarse salt. This will create an attractive presentation for the scallop shells and prevent them from sliding on the plate. Set aside.

Using an oyster knife or small, strong (but not sharp) knife, carefully pry open the shells. Run the knife under the bottom shell to detach the scallop. Scoop out the scallop, discarding the white muscles and the dark organs and keeping the orange coral in place. Keep the decorative shells to use as "serving dishes." Thoroughly rinse the scallops of all sand and residue. Pat dry with paper towels and set aside.

Wash and dry the shells. Place on two large baking pans. Return the scallops to the centers of the shells. Season the white part with salt and pepper. Sprinkle the scallops with the thyme leaves, lightly dust them with the cheese and breadcrumbs, and drizzle with olive oil. Bake until the tops lightly brown, 4 to 5 minutes. Using tongs, transfer three scallops in their shells to each serving plate, lightly pressing the shells into the salt to secure them. Serve immediately.

This is one of Maurizio's favorite recipes: succulent, barely cooked oysters under a warm blanket of Parmigiano-Reggiano and crisp breadcrumbs.

Oven-Baked Oysters

Ostriche Passate al Forno   *Makes 6 servings*

Coarse salt to line baking pans and serving plates
  (about 5 pounds)
30 oysters with large shells, such as Blue Points
Freshly ground black pepper
⅓ cup unseasoned breadcrumbs, preferably fresh and
  finely ground (see page 32)
⅓ cup finely grated Parmigiano-Reggiano
2 tablespoons chopped chives plus 12 long chive leaves
⅓ cup (5 tablespoons) melted usalted butter
6 thin slices of lemon
6 sprigs curly parsley

Arrange the oven rack 3 to 4 inches below the broiler. Preheat the broiler. Cover the bottoms of six serving plates with about ¼ inch coarse salt. Set aside.

Cover the bottoms of two large baking pans with about 1 inch salt to prevent the oysters from tipping.

Open the oysters by placing the cupped side down on a flat surface and inserting a dull knife (preferably an oyster knife) into the hinge. Press and twist the knife inside the shell, wiggling the knife until the oyster pops open. Twist off the top shell over a bowl to catch any spilled liquid. Detach the meat from the bottom shell, then return it to the shell along with any spilled liquid. Arrange the oysters in the pans, lightly pressing them into the salt. Season with pepper, then lightly dust with the breadcrumbs and cheese and sprinkle with the chopped chives. Drizzle about ½ teaspoon of the melted butter over each oyster. Place the pans under the broiler just until the tops begin to brown, 1 to 1½ minutes. Place five oysters on each salt-covered serving plate. Place a lemon slice, attractively twisted, 2 long chive leaves, and a parsley sprig in the center and serve.

MAURIZIO SUGGESTS: A Sauvignon Blanc from Trentino–Alto Adige is a perfect match.

Baccalà

Elsewhere in Italy baccalà refers to dried salt cod, but in Venice we use air-dried, unsalted stockfish. Its use dates from the Renaissance, when a Venetian explorer returned with a Scandinavian process for preserving *stoccafisso* without salt, a costly ingredient at the time. When the Catholic Church decided that followers were to refrain from eating meat on certain holy days, rehydrated stockfish became a popular, less expensive alternative to fresh fish. By the time Venice had monopolized the salt business and the condiment was cheap and plentiful, locals preferred the air-dried preserving method, though they called the fish *baccalà*.

The best type to use is Norwegian *stoccafisso ragno*, which is the smallest, softest, and has the most delicate flavor. If you can't find it, use baccalà, or salt cod, taking care to change the water four times a day, and don't add any salt. Most of the baccalà sold in North America is still moist, which makes for a shorter soaking time. If you buy a large piece of fish (which yields a better texture than smaller ones), cut it into small pieces with kitchen shears to make soaking easier. At da Fiore, the fish is submerged in water for four days—we change the water twice daily—but you can also keep the baccalà under slowly running, constantly refreshed water, if you prefer.

This vibrant plate of four kinds of fish, three lightly "cooked" in citrus juice and each served with an individual sauce, has become da Fiore's signature dish. When Mara first tasted sushi on a trip to the United States, Maurizio encouraged her to develop a Venetian version. Rather than serving all of the fish raw, Mara discovered that bass is best when marinated in lemon juice, yet orange complements shrimp's inherent sweetness. We never marinate tuna—it's delicious on its own. Seek out the highest-quality sushi-grade tuna you can find and drizzle on a light, Ligurian olive oil. We serve it with marinated vegetables, such as radicchio (see page 56), and toasted bread.

Mediterranean-Style Ceviche

Misto Crudo di Pesce alla Mediterranea   *Makes 4 servings*

Four 10- to 12-ounce whole red mullet or
   eight 2- to 3-ounce fillets
One 2-pound sea bream or two 6-ounce fillets
Salt and freshly ground red peppercorns
9 lemons, halved
4 medium shrimp, peeled and deveined
Juice of 4 oranges
4 thin slices tuna (about 4 ounces)
1 tablespoon chopped flat-leaf parsley

Caper and Thyme Sauce
¼ cup extra virgin olive oil
½ tablespoon capers
1 teaspoon chopped thyme

Rosemary Sauce
1 cup extra virgin olive oil
1 teaspoon crushed hot red pepper
1 tablespoon chopped rosemary
1 garlic clove, minced

Wild Fennel or Dill Sauce

1 cup extra virgin olive oil
2 tablespoons chopped wild fennel (substitute dill if
   unavailable)
¼ cup fresh lemon juice
1 hot red pepper, seeded and minced

Onion Sauce

¼ cup extra virgin olive oil
1 tablespoon minced red onion or shallot
1 tablespoon balsamic vinegar
Juice of 1 orange

If using whole red mullet and sea bream, remove the scales and fillet the fish (see page 10). Leave the red mullet fillets whole. Cut the sea bream fillets in half on the diagonal.

Season the red mullet and sea bream with salt and pepper and place in a square or rectangular glass dish just large enough to hold the fillets in one layer. Squeeze the juice from all but two lemon halves into the dish. Marinate for 30 minutes.

Place the shrimp and the orange juice in a small bowl. Set aside for 10 minutes.

Meanwhile, prepare the sauces to top the fish. In the work bowl of a mini food processor or using a hand-held blender, blend together the ingredients for each sauce; rinse the bowl between preparations and reserve each separately.

Remove the fish from the lemon marinade and the shrimp from the orange juice and pat dry with paper towels. On each serving plate, place a red mullet fillet, a piece of sea bream, a slice of tuna, and a shrimp. Drizzle the rosemary sauce over the red mullet; thyme and caper sauce over the tuna; wild fennel sauce over the sea bream; and onion sauce over the shrimp. Add chopped parsley over each dish. Serve with an aromatic toasted bread, such as rosemary or olive peasant bread.

MAURIZIO SUGGESTS: A bone-dry, aromatic white with moderate acidity and lightly bitterish aftertaste, such as a dry Moscato from Colli Euganei Veneti.

A dark green tangle of slightly wilted puntarelle topped with a fan of thinly sliced striped bass is da Fiore's signature winter salad. Puntarelle, the sweet-tempered chicory that comes to market when the weather gets cold, tastes intensely bitter at first. Soaking the foot-long, leafy fronds in several changes of ice water rids them of their abrasive edge.

Assemble this dish an hour or so in advance and simply warm it before serving. The fish's temperature should be tepid—just enough to release the puntarelle's herbaceous aroma.

Warm Striped Bass with Puntarelle Salad

Tiepido di Branzino *Makes 6 servings*

1 large bunch puntarelle (about 1 pound)
1½ pounds striped bass fillets
3 whole anchovies, salt- or oil-packed
⅓ cup plus 2 tablespoons extra virgin olive oil
1 garlic clove, quartered
2 tablespoons red wine vinegar
Salt and freshly ground black pepper
2 tablespoons chopped chives plus 12 long chive leaves
¼ cup fine fresh breadcrumbs (see page 32)

To clean the puntarelle, remove the long outside leaves from each stem until you arrive at the thick stem base (heart) in the center. Reserve the outer leaves for another use, such as braising or mixing with salad greens. Trim and discard the hard end from the bottom of each stem, about 2 inches. Slice each stem into 4-inch segments, then cut lengthwise into julienne strips. Put the puntarelle in a large bowl of ice water; set aside for 4 hours. Change the ice water at least three times to remove the bitterness of the puntarelle. Drain and spin dry. Place the puntarelle in a medium bowl. Set aside.

Using a fish knife, cut the bass on the diagonal into approximately 28 thin slices, ⅛ to ¼ inch thick. Overlap the slices slightly on a plate; cover and refrigerate until you're ready to assemble the salad.

Using a small knife, scrape any visible bones from the anchovies and rinse well. Pat dry between paper towels. Set aside.

Heat a small skillet with the ⅓ cup olive oil and the garlic over medium heat. Cook until the garlic is golden, about 3 minutes. Discard the garlic and add the anchovies to the skillet. Using a fork, mash the anchovies into the oil. Lower the heat to medium-low and cook, stirring, until smooth, about 2 minutes.

Remove the skillet from the heat, stir in the vinegar, and season with salt and pepper. Whisk to emulsify the ingredients. When the dressing cools slightly, pour in the chopped chives, then pour over the puntarelle; toss to combine. Mound the puntarelle in the centers of six heatproof salad plates. Set aside.

Preheat the broiler on high setting.

Drape five to six slices of the bass, overlapping slightly, on top of the puntarelle to form a cap with no exposed green. Season the fish with salt and pepper. Lightly dust with the breadcrumbs and the chives. Drizzle with the remaining olive oil. Form an X over the top of each dish by crisscrossing two of the long chive leaves. Place under the broiler and cook until the fish lightly browns, 3 to 5 minutes, depending on the intensity of the broiler. Turn the plates as necessary during cooking to promote even browning. Serve immediately, placing the hot salad plate on an underplate. Be sure to advise your guests that the salad plates are hot.

Breadcrumbs, Croutons, and Crostini

BREADCRUMBS ARE INDISPENSABLE in our kitchen. A light coating of breadcrumbs preserves the color and the texture of fish fillets as they cook.

Arrange cubes of day-old bread on a sheet pan and bake on low heat (200°F) in the oven until they dry—about three hours. Place the dried bread in the bowl of a food processor with the steel blade and process until the crumbs are as fine as semolina or coarse polenta. We season breadcrumbs as needed. Since we always have leftover bread, we make fresh breadcrumbs every day, but they can be kept for a week if stored in the refrigerator.

To make croutons and crostini, cut large slices, cubes, or wedges of day-old bread and bake the same way at 200°F.

When marinated in fresh lemon juice, bass, with its lean, meaty taste, transforms from translucent to pearly white, creating a striking canvas for the bright green herb sauce. Marinate the fish for no longer than two hours or else it will become mushy.

Marinated Striped Bass with Aromatic Herbs

Branzino Marinato alle Erbe Aromatiche   *Makes 4 servings*

2 striped bass fillets with skin (about 1 pound total)
9 lemons, halved (to yield about 1¼ cups juice)
¾ cup extra virgin olive oil
½ small onion, thinly sliced
2 tablespoons chopped marjoram leaves
1 tablespoon thyme leaves
1½ teaspoons cumin seeds
Salt and freshly ground red peppercorns

Rinse the bass fillets, pat dry, and place skin side up in a square or rectangular glass dish just large enough to hold the fillets in one layer. Squeeze the juice into the dish from all but one lemon half and season with salt. Cover and marinate, refrigerated, for 2 hours.

Meanwhile, prepare the aromatic herb sauce. Heat ¼ cup of the olive oil in a small saucepan over medium heat. Add the onion and cook until soft, about 5 minutes. One by one, add the marjoram, thyme, and cumin seeds, cooking for 30 seconds after each addition. Add the juice from the remaining lemon half, about a tablespoon; cook for another minute, then remove the pan from the heat. Whisk in the remaining olive oil and season with salt and pepper. Set aside.

Remove the fish from the marinade. Lightly pat dry with paper towels. Using a sharp knife, thinly slice the fillets crosswise on the diagonal, overlapping them slightly on serving plates or a serving platter as you cut them. Spoon the herb sauce over the fish. Serve with warm bread or crostini.

The ingredient that gives this glorious antipasto its rich aroma and luxurious taste and texture is invisible to the naked eye. As you bite into these sweet, succulent scampi on crisp crostini, the only clue that they've been draped in aromatic lard is the glossy melted topping.

Instead of butter and oil, which is used more commonly today, Venetians used to prefer *lardo* (fat rendered from pigs), especially in desserts, since its taste is much lighter. This *lardo* is entirely different from American lard sold in buckets or bars. Artisanally produced, the pork fat is generously seasoned with herbs such as rosemary and aged to develop its characteristic rich flavor and creamy texture. We're partial to Lardo di Collonata or di Varzi; when melted, the *profumo* is unforgettable! If you can't find seasoned *lardo* at a specialty food store, substitute slices of pancetta (unsmoked, salt-cured pig belly) for a meatier dimension. In a pinch, any unsmoked bacon can be used. If scampi or langoustine are unavailable, use large shrimp. If the shrimp are very large, lower the temperature in the oven to allow them to cook through without burning the other ingredients.

Crostini with Scampi in Lard and Rosemary

Crostini di Scampi al Lardo e Rosmarino   *Makes 6 servings*

4 thin slices sandwich bread
8 ounces lard with rind, cold (preferably salt and pepper
   cured) or pancetta
Leaves from 1 sprig rosemary
16 scampi (langoustine) or large shrimp, peeled and deveined
4 cherry tomatoes
5 tablespoons grated Parmigiano-Reggiano

Fried Rosemary (optional garnish)
Corn or sunflower oil for frying
6 sprigs rosemary
¼ recipe da Fiore Batter (page 59)
Salt

Preheat the oven to 450°F.

Cut each slice of bread into four wedges and place on a baking pan. Remove the rind from the lard, then cut into 16 long, thin pieces. Lay the lard on a cutting board and sprinkle with the rosemary leaves (2 to 3 leaves per slice). Top the end of each piece with a langoustine or shrimp. Roll the langoustine in the lard and place over a bread slice on the baking pan.

Using a sharp knife, slice an X on the stem top of each cherry tomato. Place the tomatoes on the baking pan with the shrimp and sprinkle the cheese over each tomato. Place the pan in the oven and bake until the shrimp is slightly firm to the touch and just cooked, about 5 minutes.

If preparing the fried rosemary, heat 3 inches of oil in a large, heavy saucepan or Dutch oven over medium heat until a deep-fat thermometer registers 350°F. Dip the rosemary sprigs in the batter, gently shaking off any excess. Fry the rosemary until crisp and golden, about 2 minutes; season with salt.

Place four crostini on each plate, arranging them so that their tips meet. Top each crostini with a shrimp and place a cherry tomato and a sprig of fried rosemary, if using, in the center. Serve immediately.

MAURIZIO SUGGESTS: A dry, full-bodied white, preferably with a bitter-almond aftertaste, such as Tocai Friulano.

Cheese, Please

AT DA FIORE, guests are often surprised to find that Mara uses cheese in many of her fish dishes. They tell us that they always thought the combination was considered "un-Italian." Elsewhere in Italy, that may be the case, but not in Venice. While there are certain traditional recipes to which cheese is never added, such as a robust *broeto,* there are few hard and fast rules forbidding such pairings in the Veneto. Parmigiano-Reggiano works well with briny oysters, but very salty seafood such as clams just tastes wrong with cheese. Soft, fresh cheeses such as mozzarella and scamorza go beautifully with sweet crustaceans.

Mara inherited this da Fiore favorite from her grandmother, who always prepared these mussels when cooking for large crowds. The secret ingredient is the brandy, which adds a sweet, oaky richness to this dish. Serve with lots of crusty bread for sopping up the broth.

da Fiore Steamed Mussels

Saltata di Cozze alla Fiore   *Makes 6 servings*

3 pounds small cultivated mussels, such as
    Prince Edward Island mussels
¼ cup extra virgin olive oil
1 garlic clove, crushed
4 plum tomatoes, peeled, seeded, and coarsely chopped or
    one 14½-ounce can whole plum tomatoes, drained
¼ cup brandy
¼ cup chopped basil leaves
2 tablespoons chopped flat-leaf parsley
Salt and freshly ground black pepper

Scrub the mussels, discarding any with broken shells and any whose shells remain open after being tapped lightly. As you clean them under cold running water, pull off the "beard," the grassy growth at the bottoms of the shells.

Heat the olive oil in a large saucepan over medium heat. Add the garlic and cook until it turns golden; remove and discard. Increase the heat to medium-high and add the mussels to the pan. Cook, stirring and turning them for 1 to 2 minutes, then cover the pan. Steam, shaking the saucepan frequently, until the mussels open, 8 to 10 minutes. Add the tomatoes, brandy, basil, and parsley; season with salt and pepper. Cook for another 5 minutes, uncovered, allowing the sauce to thicken slightly. Divide among six bowls and serve immediately with garlic-rubbed crostini (see page 32) or slices of bread.

MAURIZIO SUGGESTS: A pleasantly aromatic white wine with good acidity, such as Gewürztraminer.

Sweet and sour, crunchy and soft, hot and cold—this colorful salad celebrates its contrasts. Tiny, translucent baby red mullet called *bianchetti* are quickly "scalded" over high heat to retain their shape and delicate taste, then are refreshed in a sweet and tart citrus salad. We love the tangy, blood-red oranges that arrive every winter, but navel oranges are a sweeter and more accessible option. Since these minuscule mullets (which are indigenous to Liguria) aren't available in North America, use tiny fresh fish such as whitebait or farmed troutlings no more than half an inch long.

Sautéed Baby Red Mullet with Blood Orange Segments

Insalate di Arance e Bianchetti Scottati *Makes 6 servings*

6 small blood or navel oranges
3 cups tender baby greens (about 5 ounces), or a mesclun mix
3 small young leeks (white and pale green parts only),
    very thinly sliced
3 Italian long, sweet green peppers, thinly sliced
6 tablespoons extra virgin olive oil
Salt and freshly ground black pepper
1 pound *bianchetti* (baby red mullet), or other tiny fish
    substitute (see headnote)
1 bunch chives, snipped into ¼-inch-long pieces

Carefully peel the oranges, removing all the bitter white pith and completely exposing the bright red flesh. Using a paring knife, remove the segments from the membrane by cutting down on each side, then lifting the segment out; transfer to a large bowl. Add the baby greens, leeks, peppers, and 3 tablespoons of the olive oil. Season with salt and pepper; gently stir to combine. Divide the mixture in neat mounds among six salad plates. Set aside.

In a medium skillet, heat the remaining 3 tablespoons olive oil over medium-high heat. Add the fish and cook for 2 minutes, gently stirring here and there. Add the chives, season with salt and pepper, and cook for another 2 minutes. Sprinkle the fish on top of the salad mixtures. Serve immediately.

This recipe was inspired by one that Mara found in an old Venetian cookbook. At first glance, it doesn't look much different from other *saors*, or sweet-and-sour marinades that have been popular in Venice for centuries. This version is called "Marco Polo" because its distinguishing ingredient—ginger—was brought to Venice after the explorer's travels in China. Citrus juices are used instead of vinegar, and leeks in place of onions, resulting in a lighter, brighter dish. Raisins and pine nuts are traditional additions to *saors*—here, Mara uses sweet, golden raisins to underscore the spiciness of the ginger.

Since *oratine* aren't available in North America, substitute the common sea bream or porgy, which are the same species and work just as well. A two-pound fish can be cut into four 6-ounce fillets by your fishmonger. Each fillet is then cut into thirds for frying. Like all *saors*, this one needs at least twelve hours to marinate, making it a perfect do-ahead dish. It can be kept in the refrigerator for five days, pulled out at the last minute, and served with broiled or grilled polenta squares.

Sweet and Sour Sea Bream Marco Polo

Saor di Oratine alla Marco Polo *Makes 6 servings*

Corn or sunflower oil for frying
Two 2-pound sea bream, or four 6-ounce sea bream fillets
    (with skin)
Salt and freshly ground black pepper
1 cup all-purpose flour
½ cup extra virgin olive oil
2 pounds leeks, white and light green parts only, thinly sliced
¾ cup pine nuts
¾ cup raisins, preferably sultanas
¾ cup water
Juice of 2 oranges
Juice of 1 lemon
1 tablespoon pickled ginger, thinly sliced

Fill a Dutch oven or deep-fat fryer with enough oil to come halfway up the sides, at least 3 inches deep. Heat the oil over medium heat until a deep-fat thermometer registers 350°F (very hot, but not smoking).

If using whole sea bream, remove the scales and fillet the fish (see page 10). Cut the fillets crosswise on the diagonal into thirds. Season each 2-ounce fillet with salt and pepper and dredge in flour. Gently shake off any excess flour.

Fry the fish in the oil until golden. Cook the fillets in two batches, if necessary, to prevent crowding, and, using a fork or tongs, turn the fillets as they cook to brown evenly. Transfer the fish to a paper towel–lined sheet pan once cooked.

To prepare the *saor*, heat the ½ cup olive oil in a medium saucepan set over medium heat. Add the leeks and cook, stirring often. When they begin to soften, about 5 minutes, add the pine nuts and raisins and season with salt. Cook, stirring, for 2 to 3 minutes, then add the water. Bring to a boil, then reduce the heat and simmer for 30 minutes. Add the orange and lemon juices and the ginger and cook until only a couple of tablespoons liquid remain, 20 to 30 minutes. Remove the pan from the heat; let cool slightly.

On the bottom of a small square or rectangular serving dish (glass or ceramic), arrange a layer of the cooked fish and top with half the *saor*. Place another layer of fish and cover with the remaining *saor*. Cover and refrigerate for at least 12 hours. Serve at room temperature with pieces of grilled or pan-seared wedges of polenta (see page 13).

A Sweet and "Saor" Tradition

IL LIBRO PER CUOCO, a fourteenth-century cookbook written anonymously in early Venetian dialect, teaches cooks how to use the new spices imported from the East. The book introduces the first-ever recipe for *Savore,* or what is now known as the sweet/sour technique called *saor.* Before refrigeration, cooks depended on these marinades to preserve fish and meat for weeks at a time.

When *saors* were at their height of popularity during the Renaissance, Venetians of every class enjoyed them. Noble families preserved more delicately flavored fish, such as sole and flounder, while the poorer classes relied on the abundant supply of inexpensive sardines. Today, with all class considerations cast aside, sardines survive as Venice's most popular *saor* preparation, found in every cicheti bar and osteria across town.

These fried sardines, marinated in vinegar and onions and sweetened with raisins, are a classic Venetian cicheti, or snack. The fish needs to marinate for at least two days and keeps for a week in the refrigerator. Serve this the traditional way—at room temperature—to best appreciate its full flavor. If you prefer your fish warm, place an oven-safe dish in a preheated oven until the sardines are warm.

Venetian-Style Sweet and Sour Sardines

Sarde in Saor   *Makes 4 servings*

½ cup seedless raisins
½ cup white wine
Corn or sunflower oil for frying
12 sardines (about 2 pounds), scaled and gutted
½ cup all-purpose flour
Salt
½ cup olive oil
4 medium white onions (about 1 pound),
    sliced into thin rings
¼ cup white wine vinegar
¾ cup pine nuts

Place the raisins in a small bowl. Cover with the white wine and let stand 30 minutes. Drain and set aside.

Fill a deep cast-iron skillet, Dutch oven, or deep-fat fryer with enough oil to come halfway up the sides, at least 3 inches deep. Place over medium heat and bring the oil to 350°F (very hot, but not smoking).

Remove the heads from the sardines, then thoroughly rinse under cold running water; pat dry with paper towels.

Working in batches of about six and holding the sardines at the head end to avoid breaking them, dredge them in flour to coat completely. Gently shake off excess flour. Fry, turning once, until golden,

3 to 4 minutes. With a slotted spoon transfer the sardines to paper towels to drain. Lightly season with salt. Set aside.

To prepare the *saor*, heat the ½ cup olive oil in a large skillet set over medium-low heat. Add the onions and cook, stirring often, until they lightly brown. Add the vinegar, adjust the heat to medium-low, and continue cooking until the onions are very soft but still have their form, about 10 minutes. Stir in the raisins and pine nuts and cook for another minute. Remove the pan from the heat; let cool slightly.

On the bottom of a small square or rectangular serving dish (glass or ceramic), arrange a layer of the cooked sardines. Top with half the *saor.* Place another layer of fish and cover with the remaining *saor;* the sardines should be completely covered. Refrigerate for at least 2 days. Serve at room temperature.

Il Redentore

*L*A FESTA DEL REDENTORE, the Feast of the Redeemer, celebrates the end of Venice's long battle with plague in 1577, which claimed a third of its population. Every year, on the third weekend in July, the festivities sprawl across the lagoon with a literal bridge of boats that stretches from Piazza San Marco to Palladio's church of il Redentore on Giudecca. On Saturday evening, families and friends row out for a picnic supper of *sarde in saor* to watch a fireworks display. The festivities continue the next day with a regatta in the lagoon.

These golden spirals, or *involtini*, of oven-roasted sardines are a favorite antipasti at da Fiore. Capers and lemon are a classic combination for fish, but not always in Venice, where the tiny berries from southern Italy are often considered too strong to partner with delicate fish. Sardines, the dark-fleshed *pesce azzurro* (the name we use for all oily fish), are abundant in the waters just outside the lagoon and stand up to the lemon-caper challenge in this simple salad. We prefer a soft Ligurian oil and a sturdy mix of greens that won't wilt too quickly when the hot dressing is drizzled over the top. This recipe can be prepared a few hours ahead; just reheat the pan juices and pour over the *involtini* before serving.

Rolled Sardines with Capers and Lemon

Involtini di Sarde con Capperi e Limone *Makes 6 servings*

18 large sardines, 5 to 6 inches long each (3 pounds total),
   scaled and gutted
Salt and freshly ground black pepper
1 small red onion, thinly sliced
3 tablespoons capers, packed in salt
4 tablespoons chopped flat-leaf parsley
Juice of 1½ lemons
2 garlic cloves, minced
¼ cup extra virgin olive oil
1 pound mixed baby greens

Fresh sardines are usually sold gutted with their heads on. Remove their heads with a knife, rinse the sardines thoroughly, gently rubbing the scales off, and pat dry with paper towels. If the sardines have not been gutted, remove the head, then run your finger from the fish's throat to the rear, scooping out the innards as you pull down with your finger. Thoroughly rinse under cold running water, gently rubbing the scales off; pat dry.

Flatten the sardines, skin side down, on a clean work surface. Lightly season with salt and pepper. Place 2 thin onion rings over each sardine. Scatter a bit of the capers, parsley, lemon juice, and garlic over each fillet. Roll each sardine from the head end to the tail end and secure with a wooden toothpick.

Into a skillet just large enough to hold the sardines in one layer, pour just enough olive oil to cover the bottom. Add the sardines and sprinkle with any remaining onions, garlic, parsley, capers, and lemon juice. Cover the skillet and cook over low heat until the sardines are just cooked and have released their flavorful juices in the bottom of the pan, 8 to 10 minutes. You may need to add a few tablespoons of water to the pan to be sure there are enough pan juices to drizzle over the sardines.

To serve, mound the greens neatly on six salad plates. Place three sardines with their ends touching to form a star on top of the greens. Whisk the pan juices and drizzle over the sardines. Serve warm or at room temperature, garnished with thin rings of the remaining red onions.

Strong Flavors, the Venetian Way

ALTHOUGH VENETIAN COOKING is one of the most delicate on the Italian peninsula, Mara doesn't shy away from boldly flavored ingredients. In fact, she softens two of the most prominent ones with these simple techniques:

Garlic: Many of Mara's dishes contain garlic, although you can hardly taste it. Before adding any other ingredients to the pot, Mara sweats two cloves of garlic in olive oil over low heat, gently draining out the flavor, then removes the cloves with a slotted spoon just as they start turning golden. That little bit of flavor is all you need.

Onions: Our local Chioggia onions are prized for their delicate flavor—the golden, sweet ones are used in our *bigoli* sauce, and the white, more robust ones are featured in the *saor* marinades. Mara often uses *cipolle di Tropea,* red onions from the southern Italian coast, for their sweet, crisp flavor.

For soups and sauces, Mara thinly slices onions using a mandoline on its finest setting. She places them in a colander. Using her fingers, she covers the slices generously in fine sea salt and leaves them to drain for two hours. During this time, the onion flavor softens and sweetens. Before cooking with them, Mara washes the onions under a steady stream of cold water for a good while to remove most of their saltiness.

Our local spider crabs are the most ungainly-looking creatures from the Mediterranean deep, but we forgive them their bad looks since their gangly legs and spiny carapaces contain the sweetest, most delectable crabmeat. Mara spends a full half hour picking away at every crevice and cranny of each crab shell, making sure not to miss a single shred, and showcases the meat in this traditional Venetian recipe, updated with a robust mayonnaise spiked with the crab roe.

It's difficult to replicate the flavor of our spider crabs outside of Venice. Although they're in the same family as king crabs, their flavor and size is much closer to Dungeness crabs from the Pacific coast. When purchasing live crabs, pick out lively specimens. The heavier they are for their size, the more meat they will contain. Or, if you don't mind missing the earthy taste of the coral in the mayonnaise, use fresh lump crabmeat.

Spider Crab with Coral Sauce

Granseola con Salsa di Corallo   *Makes 8 servings*

Coarse salt
8 live female Granseola crabs (about 10 ounces each), or
   6 live Dungeness crabs (about 1¼ pounds each)
2 large eggs
2 cups extra virgin olive oil
Juice of 1 lemon plus 8 thin lemon slices
Salt and freshly ground black pepper
8 sprigs curly parsley

Bring a large pot of water to a boil. Generously season with coarse salt. Add the crabs to the boiling water and cook, partially covered, for 15 minutes; they should be bright red. Drain and set aside to cool. Scrub the outside of the crabs, using a stiff brush. Rinse.

Remove the legs; set aside. Peel the belly shell from each crab; rinse thoroughly and reserve—these will be the "serving bowls." Using a small blunt knife and your fingers when necessary, remove the bright red coral (eggs) and the yellowish brown paste from the body; transfer to a bowl. Work the paste through your fingers to detect and discard any pieces of hard cartilage. Set aside. Using a large chef's knife, cut the crab lengthwise in half. Cut off the hard stubs where the legs were connected—this will help in extracting the meat. Cut the crab in half again crosswise. Using a long wooden skewer, scrape the meat from all four sections of the crab body into a separate bowl. To remove the meat from the

crab legs, give each of the three segments one firm hit with a flat-bottomed mallet to crack the shell. (Repeated strikes should be avoided, as they will cause splintering, and shell fragments will be mixed with the meat.) Using your hands, transfer the large pieces of meat to the bowl. Use a wooden skewer or toothpick to remove the rest. Add 2 tablespoons of the reserved coral mixture to the bowl; gently stir to combine. Portion the crabmeat into the reserved shell bowls.

To prepare the sauce, place the eggs in a food processor. Turn on the machine and drizzle the olive oil through the feed tube in a thin, steady stream. After you have added about half the oil, the mixture will thicken; you can add the remaining oil more quickly. Turn the machine off. Add the remaining coral mixture and the lemon juice and season with salt and pepper. Process until smooth. Divide the sauce among eight small ramekins or serving bowls.

To serve, roll two ends of clean cloth napkins (preferably white or cream colored) inward a few inches to form two side walls; repeat, creating eight in total. Set a prepared napkin on a serving plate. Place a crab-filled shell and the sauce on each plate. Garnish the top of the crabmeat with a lemon slice and parsley sprig. Serve immediately.

Traghetti

*U*NTIL THE TWENTIETH CENTURY, the only bridge that crossed the Grand Canal was the famous stone Ponte Rialto. Until the Ponte Scalzi and Ponte Accademia were built, Venetians traveled in traghetti to get to the other side. They remain the most efficient way to cross the Grand Canal from eleven different locations. Traghetti are gondolas that hold up to fourteen standing passengers. A trip costs about fifty cents, and although they only operate in daylight, they're much more exciting than the huge *vaporetti* (water buses) that buzz around the Grand Canal. Look for the yellow TRAGHETTO signs that point toward the canal, or refer to any official Venetian map, where the traghetti routes are marked.

"Are they here yet?" It's a question Venetians ask every autumn when the waters run cold in the lagoon. Just half an inch long at most, with a subtle sweetness and tender texture, *schie,* tiny brown shrimp (which don't turn pink when cooked) were once a staple of *la cucina povera,* or the cooking of the poor. Nowadays, all of Venice clamors for them in the late fall and early winter. *Schie* are traditionally sautéed in a rich parsley-garlic sauce, and served on top of polenta, but Maurizio suggests placing the sauced *schie* on one side of the plate and the polenta on the other, the better to appreciate the distinct flavors of each. *Schie* are rarely shipped outside of our lagoon, but this recipe can be reproduced with the small, sweet titi shrimp from Indonesia, or use the smallest shrimp you can find.

Adriatic Brown Shrimp with Soft Polenta

Schie con Polenta   *Makes 6 servings*

1 recipe soft polenta (page 13)
3 pounds small shrimp (no more than half an inch long)
Coarse salt
¾ cup extra virgin olive oil
¾ cup chopped flat-leaf parsley
2 garlic cloves, halved
Freshly ground black pepper

Begin the polenta 20 to 30 minutes before boiling the shrimp.

Bring about 6 quarts of water to a boil. Generously season with coarse salt. Add the shrimp, stir to disperse, then cover the pan. When the water returns to a boil, the shrimp are cooked; immediately drain through a colander and set aside. When the shrimp are cool enough to handle, pull off the heads and shells. The shells can be discarded or kept for a broth.

Combine the olive oil, parsley, and garlic in a small bowl. Add the shrimp, season with pepper, and stir to combine. Set the mixture aside to marinate for 15 minutes.

To serve, generously spoon the warm soft polenta on the side of each serving plate. Using a slotted spoon, arrange the cooked shrimp next to the polenta. Stir the parsley sauce and drizzle it over the shrimp. Serve immediately.

In Venice and the Veneto, we boast countless radicchio recipes, but this is one of our favorites. Pickled in wine and vinegar, infused with the warmth of clove and cinnamon, it's delicious with raw fish *crudi* or on its own as an antipasto. Radicchio's inherent bitterness lessens when cooked, but in this recipe, a dry white table wine makes it sweet. Use a Tuscan oil with a bit of a bite for contrast. Stored in an airtight container in the refrigerator, this will last for two weeks.

Marinated Radicchio di Treviso

Radicchio di Treviso Marinato   *Makes 6 servings*

12 heads radicchio di Treviso (about 8 inches long)
1 quart water
One 750-ml bottle dry white wine
2 tablespoons red wine vinegar
10 whole cloves
2 cinnamon sticks
2 tablespoons coarse salt
About 2 cups extra virgin olive oil

Remove any limp outer leaves from the radicchio. Starting at the tips, cut the radicchio crosswise into 1-inch slices. When you get to the white stem, cut it into quarters. Rinse well and drain.

Line a baking pan with a clean kitchen towel and set aside.

Combine a quart of water, the white wine, vinegar, cloves, cinnamon, and salt in a medium saucepan. Bring to a boil. Add half the radicchio, return the cooking liquid to a low boil, and cook for 8 minutes, until slightly tender and "pickled." Using a slotted spoon, transfer the radicchio to the towel-lined baking pan. Repeat with the remaining radicchio. When cool, loosely cover and set aside to "dry" for 12 hours. Transfer the radicchio to an airtight container; add enough extra virgin olive oil to cover. Store for up to two weeks in a cool, dry place or refrigerated.

A few years ago, Mara set out to create a festive dish to highlight Venice's superb seasonal vegetables. A reinterpretation of fritto misto came to her mind, and the first challenge was the batter. Traditional Venetian batters are heavy and often oily, so Mara created a lighter tempura-style one.

Here, summer vegetables are featured, but in the spring, Mara cooks asparagus and baby artichokes. In the fall, we add slices of pumpkin and wild mushrooms from the country. Winter brings broccoli and cauliflower, some radicchio, fennel, and even orange slices.

Salt, drain, and dry the zucchini and eggplant first, or else they'll absorb too much oil when frying. We slice firmer vegetables, such as pumpkin and broccoli, smaller than the others, parboil them, and cook them in the oil first. The light, clean flavor of sunflower oil, which is available at specialty food stores in North America, is our first choice for frying, but corn oil is a fine substitution. Always attach a thermometer to the fryer to maintain the proper temperature. As you add the vegetables, the temperature will drop down a bit and you'll have to wait until it climbs back to 350°F to add more.

Fried Seasonal Vegetables da Fiore

Fritto di Verdure di Stagione   *Makes 6 servings*

3 medium carrots, peeled

1 medium eggplant

3 medium zucchini

1½ tablespoons coarse salt

1 tablespoon chopped marjoram

1 tablespoon chopped thyme

1 tablespoon chopped rosemary

1 green bell pepper, cored, seeded, and sliced
    into 6 long pieces

1 red bell pepper, cored, seeded, and sliced into 6 long pieces

1 yellow bell pepper, cored, seeded, and sliced
    into 6 long pieces

3 medium onions (red or white), cut into ¼-inch-thick rings

6 zucchini flowers

Flour for dredging

6 mint sprigs as garnish

da Fiore Batter
3 cups all-purpose flour
5 cups water
2 teaspoons salt
6 ice cubes
Corn or sunflower oil for frying

Cut the carrots and eggplant in half crosswise. Using a sharp knife or a mandoline, slice the halves and the whole zucchini lengthwise into ⅛- to ¼-inch-thick pieces. Spread the eggplant and zucchini slices, separately, around the bottom and sides of a large colander and sprinkle with a tablespoon of the salt and half the marjoram, thyme, and rosemary. Place the colander over a bowl and let stand for 30 minutes. Place the carrot slices on a large sheet pan along with the peppers and onions. Season with the remaining ½ tablespoon salt and herbs. Set aside for an hour, allowing the water to drain from the vegetables.

Meanwhile, prepare the batter. In a medium bowl, whisk together the flour, water, and salt to form a smooth, thin batter. Stir in the ice cubes. Set aside for at least 30 minutes. Before using the batter, add a few more ice cubes and thin with a little water if necessary.

In a large heavy saucepan or Dutch oven, heat 3 inches oil over medium heat until a deep-fat thermometer registers 350°F. Place the flour for dredging in a bowl.

Working in batches to prevent crowding, dip the vegetables, including the zucchini flowers, in a bowl of water, then dredge in flour, shaking off any excess. Dip in the batter, letting the excess drip off, and fry until deep golden, 2 to 3 minutes. Transfer the vegetables to a paper towel–lined sheet pan as they cook and season with salt if desired. Serve a mixture of vegetables topped with a fresh mint sprig.

Since there's only one *castraure*, or baby artichoke in the center of each plant, they are among the most prized of all Venetian vegetables. When these tender delicacies come to market in March each year, we celebrate with this colorful salad. Blood oranges add a sweet acidity that tempers the artichokes' bitter edge. These artichokes call for a bracing oil, so if you have a Tuscan olive oil on hand, use it. As with most salads, Mara finds mixing spoons useless. Dive in fingers first—it's the only way to completely dress a salad, especially given artichokes' nooks and crannies.

Our *castraure* are so tiny that they're choke-less and tender, which means you can enjoy them raw. The same is true for the "baby" artichokes available across the United States, which are sold before they've had a chance to develop a choke (or too much of one).

Baby Artichokes with Oranges and Parmigiano Shavings

Castraure con Arance e Parmigiano   *Makes 6 servings*

3 blood or navel oranges
18 baby artichokes
Juice of 1 lemon
3 tablespoons extra virgin olive oil
2 tablespoons chopped flat-leaf parsley
Salt and freshly ground black pepper
6 ounces Parmigiano-Reggiano, thinly shaved
   with a vegetable peeler

Peel the oranges, removing all the bitter white pith. Over a small bowl to capture the juices, separate the segments from the membrane by inserting a paring knife on both sides, then lifting the segment out. Squeeze any remaining juice from the segmented orange. Set the juice aside. Slice the segments in half crosswise, and put in a separate bowl; set aside.

Cut the stems and the spiny tops of the leaves from the artichokes. Starting at the base, bend the leaves back and snap them off where they break naturally; continue until all tough outer leaves have been removed, leaving a cone of tender pale green leaves. Using a small sharp knife, trim the outside edge of the base until smooth and no dark green areas remain. As you work, place the cleaned artichokes in a bowl; cover with water and squeeze in the lemon juice to prevent browning.

One by one, cut the artichokes in half lengthwise. Using a small knife, cut out any choke (there will be very little in baby artichokes) and small purple-tipped leaves from each halve. Slice the cleaned artichoke halves as thinly as possible and place them in a large bowl. Add the juice from the oranges, the olive oil, and parsley, and season with salt and pepper. Mix to combine. Using your hands, gently mix in the orange segments.

To serve, divide the salad among six plates, top with a few shavings of the cheese, and drizzle with extra virgin olive oil.

MAURIZIO SUGGESTS: A glass of cold water! Artichokes have a tannic taste, which makes them difficult to pair with wine. When we finish eating this dish, we usually eat a piece of bread and take a few more sips of water to clean the palate, then move on to the next course.

Rich, creamy custards date back to Venetian courtly traditions, when elegant puddings were unmolded with formal flourishes on extravagant, silver-laid tables. When spring's first asparagus appears, this dish appears on da Fiore's menu.

Asparagus and Parmigiano Custard

Budino di Parmigiano-Reggiano con Asparagi Gratinati   *Makes 6 to 8 servings*

Unsalted butter for greasing the pan
4 large eggs
2 tablespoons all-purpose flour
2½ cups (8 ounces) grated Parmigiano-Reggiano
   plus ½ cup (1½ ounces) shavings
1¼ cups heavy cream
1¼ cups milk
¼ teaspoon salt
1 bunch (about 1 pound) green or white asparagus,
   washed, ends trims, stems peeled

Preheat the oven to 350°F. Thoroughly grease a 6-cup Bundt pan, preferably nonstick. Set aside.

In a large bowl, beat the eggs and the flour together. Add the Parmigiano, cream, milk, and salt, mixing until well combined. Pour the custard into the prepared pan. Place the pan in a larger pan and fill with enough warm water to reach halfway up the sides of the Bundt pan. Bake in the middle of the oven until set and firm, about an hour and 10 minutes. Let rest 20 minutes in the water bath before inverting the pudding from the pan.

During the last 30 minutes of cooking/resting, prepare the asparagus. Cook the spears in a large pot of boiling, salted water until just tender, 3 to 5 minutes, depending on the thickness. Drain. Generously grease a baking dish large enough to hold the asparagus in a single layer. Top with the Parmigiano shavings and place in the oven until lightly browned, 8 to 10 minutes.

Invert the slightly warm pudding from the Bundt pan onto a decorative serving dish or platter. Arrange the cooked asparagus in the center and serve immediately.

MAURIZIO SUGGESTS: Soave Classico Superiore would be an outstanding complement.

Primi Piatti

AFTER THE ANTIPASTO PLATES ARE WHISKED AWAY, PALATES ARE POISED FOR HEARTY RISOTTOS, PASTAS, AND SOUPS. OUR *PRIMI PIATTI,* OR FIRST plates, consist of comfort classics, like traditional *risi e bisi* (rice and peas), *spaghetti con vongole veraci,* clams, and *broeto,* the hearty fishermen's stew. At da Fiore, we serve small portions to leave room for a *secondo piatto,* or second course. At home, you can serve these recipes as a *piatto unico,* or "the only dish." We often do so when preparing lunch or a light dinner for ourselves, along with a salad and bread.

Pasta

Polenta and rice may be the Veneto's traditional starches of choice, but Venetians enjoy more than their fair share of pasta as well. Fresh egg pasta, traditionally rolled out by hand and cut into long ribbons called tagliatelle, or the thinner tagliolini, is most common. We used a hand-cranked pasta roller until we discovered the motorized version—same quality, fewer arm cramps!

Dried pastas made with hard durum wheat and water also have their place at the Venetian table. At da Fiore, we use *pasta di grano duro artiginale,* which is made in the traditional way—extruded through brass dies and allowed to dry slowly. The pasta's flavor is fuller, and its slightly rough surface allows the sauce to cling to it. Artisanal pastas are widely available in specialty food stores and through mail order in North America. We cook our dried pasta al dente, or still slightly firm in the center, so keep checking and tasting as you near the end of cooking so that the pasta can be drained at the right moment.

Before da Fiore was the elegant *ristorante* that it is today, we did a swift business at the bar, serving grilled fish dinners and bite-size Venetian bar food. There was a regular guest who without fail occupied the same bar stool every night, happy to enjoy whatever fish Mara prepared that evening. He eventually asked for pasta, and one day, to his surprise, Mara brought out this preparation—a hearty, baked tagliolini woven with stands of cooked-down radicchio and sweet baby shrimp, enriched with Parmigiano-Reggiano and cream. He couldn't have been happier, and this recipe has been on our menu ever since.

Though this may seem like a rich dish best reserved for winter evenings, try it in the summer at room temperature as well. Fresh egg tagliolini is the best pasta for this dish, but fresh fettucine or angel hair will work. Use the tight, dark red heads of radicchio di Chioggia, which aren't as bitter as other varieties and lend a lovely violet hue to the cream. Panna, a thick Italian cream that's available at many Italian markets in small cardboard containers, is Mara's favorite way to add richness without making a more labor-intensive *besciamella*. If you can't find it, heavy cream, reduced slightly, creates a binder that's just as rich and delicious.

Gratin of Tagliolini with Radicchio and Shrimp

Tagliolini con Scampi e Radicchio   *Makes 4 first-course servings*

3 tablespoons unsalted butter
¼ small onion, thinly sliced
3 cups shredded radicchio, preferably di Chioggia
½ pound large shrimp, peeled, deveined, and halved
½ cup white wine
1 cup heavy cream
Salt and freshly ground black pepper
¾ pound fresh tagliolini or fettucine
¼ cup grated Parmigiano-Reggiano

Preheat the oven to 400°F.

In a large sauté pan, heat the butter over medium heat. Add the onion, cook 1 to 2 minutes, then add the radicchio and shrimp. Cook, tossing or stirring, until the radicchio is limp, about 8 minutes. Add the white wine and cook to reduce slightly, about 2 minutes. Add the cream and cook until the sauce thickens and turns a slightly violet color from the radicchio, about 2 minutes. Season with salt and pepper. Set aside briefly.

Cook the pasta in a large pot of boiling salted water until al dente. Drain. Add the pasta to the sauce; toss or gently stir to combine. Transfer to a baking dish and sprinkle the top with the cheese. Bake until the top lightly browns, about 10 minutes. Remove the pan from the oven; let cool slightly, about 5 minutes, before serving.

MAURIZIO SUGGESTS: A dry, full-bodied white wine that isn't aged in wood, such as one of our local Chardonnays.

Radicchio: Pride of the Veneto

TREVISO PRECOCE CICORIA

RADICCHIO DI CHIOGGIA

RADICCHIO DI CASTELFRANCO

RADICCHIO DI VERONA

TREVISO TARDIVO

INSALATA RICCIA OR INDIVIA

AN ASSORTMENT *of* **RADICCHIO**

T DA FIORE, this red-leafed chicory is one of our most beloved vegetables, ever versatile and always compatible with fish. All varieties have a bitter flavor that dissipates while cooking.

Though available all year, radicchio is best in the winter, just after the green leaves turn a rich red. Radicchio is the Italian word for chicory, a term that encompasses a large family of greens, from endive to escarole. The Veneto is home to many chicories that grow in local gardens, and in the 1800s, local farmers began cultivating them. Each region rose to fame with new varieties, and now there's an official consortium dedicated to the eight communities where regional types of radicchio prosper.

The oldest and most prized variety is radicchio di Treviso. There are two harvests to look forward to: the *precoce,* or early radicchio di Treviso with its wide, mild red leaves, is available in the early fall. The *tardivo,* or later harvest, is most eagerly anticipated. In December, Mara brings huge bouquets of them into the kitchen. Most of the outer leaves have been pulled off, leaving the root at the base and a jumble of long, tender red and white stems. Their flavor is deep and assertive, and there's no better radicchio for grilling.

Radicchio rosso di Treviso is the most common variety in Venice and the one you're most likely to find tossed into salads. Its elongated head is loosely packed with dark red leaves and thick white stems, and its flavor is mild. Radicchio di Castelfranco looks more like a head of leaf lettuce; its leaves are speckled white, red, and pink. Radicchio di Chioggia, with its dark burgundy leaves and tightly packed round heads that look like miniature cabbages, are commonly found in North America, where they are often mistaken for our looser and longer radicchio di Verona.

Mara had Valentine's Day in mind when she designed this plate of saffron-laced pasta studded with gently cooked oysters. The flavors are indeed lusty, carried in a dreamy butter and leek sauce and pinned to a smoky backdrop of speck. If you can't find speck, a smoked, cured ham from the northern provinces of Italy, you can use smoked slab bacon or a *guanciale affumicato*. If you order this dish at da Fiore, you can tell that it's one of Maurizio's favorites. From a cart alongside the table, he twirls pasta strands in the butter sauce one forkful at a time before plating.

Pappardelle with Oysters and Saffron

Pappardelle con Ostriche e Zafferano   *Makes 6 first-course servings*

Fresh Pasta

3 cups all-purpose flour plus more as needed

3 extra large eggs

3 tablespoons olive oil

3 tablespoons water

1 teaspoon salt

Sauce

10 tablespoons (1¼ sticks) unsalted butter

2 leeks (white parts only), cleaned and sliced thin

5 ounces speck, diced

2 teaspoons saffron threads

36 oysters, shucked, with juice reserved

⅓ cup dry white wine

3 tablespoons chopped flat-leaf parsley

Salt and freshly ground black pepper

To prepare the pasta, place a mound of flour on a pasta board or clean work surface. Use a fork to make a center well. Put the eggs, oil, water, and salt in the well. With the fork, mix together the liquid, then begin incorporating the flour from the inside rim of the well. Continue to push the flour into the liquid ingredients, pulling the pieces of dough together with your hands; add a tablespoon or two of water if the dough is too dry, or more if using large rather than extra large eggs. Scrape the board with a pastry scraper to gather all of the dough. Knead the dough, dusting the board with flour if too moist, until you have a smooth, elastic ball of dough, about 5 minutes. Wrap the dough in plastic wrap and set aside to rest for 30 minutes.

Line a tray with clean kitchen towels. Set the pasta roller on the widest setting; cut the pasta in two pieces. Flatten each piece of dough into a rectangle and feed it through the rollers. Repeat this process eight to nine times, folding the dough in half each time and dusting with flour to prevent sticking. Cut the pasta sheets into rectangles 12-inches long. Using a plain or fluted pastry wheel, cut the sheets lengthwise at about ½-inch intervals. Sprinkle the pappardelle generously with flour. Form the pasta loosely into a nest and arrange it on the towel-lined tray. Make more pappardelle with the remaining dough in the same manner. Pappardelle may be made a day ahead and chilled on the towel-lined tray, covered loosely with plastic wrap.

Fill a large pot with water and bring to a boil.

To prepare the sauce, melt the butter in a large skillet over medium-high heat. Add the leeks, speck, and saffron and cook, stirring often, for 2 minutes. Add the oysters and their juice, cook for a minute, then add the white wine and cook for another minute, until slightly reduced. Add the parsley, season with salt and pepper, then remove from the heat.

Salt the boiling water and cook the pappardelle until tender but firm, about 3 minutes. Heat the sauce, drain the pasta, and toss in the pan. Toss to coat and serve immediately.

MAURIZIO SUGGESTS: A dry, full-bodied, aromatic white wine such as a Sauvignon dell'Alto Adige.

Although broccoli isn't native to the lagoon, farmers have recently started cultivating it here. Mara loves the way its pronounced flavor softens once cooked. Since broccoli's arrival at the market coincides with the end of Fermo Pesca, the wintertime period when the lagoon shuts down to allow the fish supply to replenish, Mara thought to pair broccoli with scallops, which are at their richest and meatiest at that time. The sweet nature of both ingredients play off each other, especially when nudged on by a little sweet paprika and buttery Parmigiano-Reggiano that create a compelling sauce. Mara's other secret: cook the pasta in the same water that the broccoli was boiled in to impart more flavor to the pennette.

Pennette with Sea Scallops and Broccoli Florets

Pennette con Cappesante e Broccoli   *Makes 6 first-course servings*

1 pound broccoli
Salt
½ pound bay scallops
¼ pound (1 stick) unsalted butter
1 small onion, chopped
2 teaspoons thyme leaves
Pinch crushed hot red pepper (optional)
Pinch sweet paprika
1 pound pennette pasta
½ cup grated Parmigiano-Reggiano

Bring a large pot of water to a boil.

Cut the florets of broccoli from the stems. Using a vegetable peeler, peel away the hard, dark green skin from the stems.

Season the water with salt and add the broccoli stems; a colander insert is helpful as the water should be retained to cook the pasta. Cook for about 8 minutes, then add the florets. Cook another 5 minutes; remove the colander insert and set aside to cool slightly. When cool enough to handle, divide the large florets into bite-size pieces and cut the stems into thin rounds. Set aside.

Rinse the scallops, removing the tough muscle if necessary. Slice the scallops crosswise into thin rounds. Pat dry with a kitchen towel.

In a large skillet, melt the butter over medium-high heat. Add the onion and cook, stirring often, until softened; do not brown. Add the scallops, thyme, and crushed red pepper, if using, and the pinch of sweet paprika. Season with salt. Cook just until the scallops change from translucent to white, 1 to 2 minutes. Add the broccoli and cook, tossing or stirring, for 2 minutes. Remove the pan from the heat.

Return the water used to cook the broccoli to a boil. Add the pennette and cook, stirring occasionally, until tender but firm.

During the last few minutes that the pasta cooks, return the skillet with the broccoli to medium-high heat. When hot, drain the pasta and add to the skillet. Toss to combine, adding the Parmigiano-Reggiano. Remove from the heat and toss again. Serve immediately.

MAURIZIO SUGGESTS: A dry white Chardonnay from the Veneto.

When da Fiore first opened in 1978 as an informal wine bar, and Mara was serving only simple platters of cicheti and grilled fish, a friend of Maurizio's came in one day craving the classic *spaghetti con vongole veraci*. Mara disappeared into the kitchen and after some time brought back a heaping plate of pasta tangled with tiny clams and fresh tomatoes. After cleaning his plate, he told Mara that it was the best he'd ever tasted, although there was one little problem: the clams were full of sand! Mara was horrified, but she quickly learned how to avoid future embarrassment. Place the clams in a bowl of salted water for an hour to flush out any sand or impurities.

Spaghetti with Clams

Spaghetti con Vongole Veraci   *Makes 4 first-course servings*

1 pound spaghetti
1 pound small manila clams, well rinsed
½ cup extra virgin olive oil
2 garlic cloves, crushed
Pinch crushed hot red pepper
4 medium tomatoes, peeled, seeded, and chopped
¼ cup dry white wine
2 tablespoons chopped flat-leaf parsley

Bring a large pot of water to a boil.

Place the clams in a medium saucepan and add ⅓ cup water. Place over medium-high heat. When the water boils, cover the pan and cook until the clams open, 4 to 5 minutes. Discard any clams that do not open. When the clams are cool enough to handle, pull the meat from the shells. Discard the shells and reserve the cooking liquid in the pan.

Salt the boiling water and add the pasta. Cook, stirring occasionally, until tender but firm. Meanwhile, in a large skillet, heat the olive oil, garlic, and crushed red pepper over medium heat. When the garlic is barely brown, add the tomato. Increase the heat to medium-high and cook, stirring occasionally, until the tomato softens, about 5 minutes. Discard the garlic. Add the clams and their juice; be sure to pour only the juice into the skillet, leaving behind any sand. Cook for a minute, then add the white wine and cook for another minute. Drain the pasta and add it to the sauce with the parsley; toss to combine. Serve immediately.

Guido Barilla, son of Barilla Pasta owner Piero Barilla, paid a great compliment to this early fall dish in a Parma newspaper, saying it had been twenty years since he felt such "incredible emotion" while eating pasta. Spoken like a true Italian. Indeed, this tastes even better than it looks, bursting with sweet strawberry grapes and tender shrimp; our guests adore it.

Uva di fragola (strawberry grapes), also called *uve Americane,* were brought over from the United States after *Phylloxera* destroyed many vineyards in the Veneto at the beginning of the last century. Seedless red globe grapes are the best substitute.

Spaghettini with Strawberry Grapes and Imperial Shrimp

Spaghettini d'Autunno con Uva di Fragola e Mazzancolle   *Makes 4 first-course servings*

¾ pound *mazzancolle* or imperial shrimp, peeled and deveined
1 cup strawberry grapes (substitute red seedless grapes)
½ cup extra virgin olive oil
1 leek (white and light green parts), cleaned and thinly sliced
½ cup white wine
4 plum tomatoes, peeled and diced
1 tablespoon chopped flat-leaf parsley
2 teaspoons snipped fresh chives
Salt and freshly ground white pepper
¾ pound spaghettini

Slice the shrimp into 1-inch pieces on the diagonal. Set aside. Cut half the grapes in half and remove any seeds. Set aside.

Heat the olive oil in a large skillet set over medium heat. Add the leek and shrimp and cook, stirring often, for 2 to 3 minutes. Add the wine and boil until reduced by about half. Add the grapes and tomatoes; cook for another minute, then stir in the parsley and chives. Add a spoonful of water if the sauce is too dry. Season with salt and pepper.

Cook the pasta in a large pot of boiling salted water. Drain and add to the skillet with the sauce. Place over medium-high heat for 1 to 2 minutes and toss or stir to combine. Serve immediately.

MAURIZIO SUGGESTS: A dry white wine with moderate acidity, such as Fiano di Avellino.

When our prized *cornetti*, thin, purplish pole beans, come to market, Mara incorporates them into a light yet robust summer pasta. The quick-cooked fresh tomato sauce with sweet mullet, light Ligurian oil, and pungent anchovies is tossed with these slender string beans, for which haricots verts or small green beans will stand in.

Spaghetti with Red Mullet Ragù, Cornetti, and Fresh Tomatoes

Spaghetti con Ragù di Triglie e Cornetti in Salsa di Pomodoro

Makes 6 first-course servings

Coarse salt
½ pound cornetti, or haricots verts, ends trimmed
    and cut into 3-inch segments
1 cup dry white wine
10 anchovy fillets
1 pound spaghetti
½ cup extra virgin olive oil
2 garlic cloves, crushed
2 medium tomatoes, peeled, seeded, and chopped
¾ pound red mullet fillets, leave whole if small
    (about 2 ounces each), cut into 3-inch pieces if large
1 tablespoon chopped flat-leaf parsley

Bring a large pot of water to a boil. Salt the water and add the haricots verts; by using a colander insert or strainer you can easily remove the beans and use the water to cook the pasta. Transfer the beans to a bowl of ice water to stop the cooking. Drain and set aside.

Pour ½ cup of the wine into a small bowl. Using a small knife, scrape any visible bones from the anchovies and rinse well in the bowl with the wine. Pat dry between paper towels. Set aside.

Cook the pasta until tender but firm.

Meanwhile, heat the olive oil and garlic in a large skillet over medium-high heat. When the garlic just starts to brown, discard and add the anchovies to the skillet. Using a fork, mash the anchovies into the oil. Lower the heat to medium-low and cook, stirring, until smooth, for about a minute. Add the haricots verts, cook for another 2 minutes, then add the tomatoes. Cook, stirring here and there, until the tomatoes soften, 3 to 4 minutes. Add the remaining white wine, cook for a moment, then add the red mullet, and cook for another 3 minutes. Add a spoonful of water if necessary to keep sauce moist. Stir in the parsley and adjust the seasoning with salt if necessary.

Drain the pasta and toss it with the sauce. Serve immediately.

MAURIZIO SUGGESTS: A dry, medium-bodied white wine that's spent some time aging in oak, such as a Pinot Bianco Colli Orientali del Friuli.

Tender lobster cooked in tomato sauce enhanced with brandy and tossed over fresh pasta ribbons—could anything be more indulgent? Use a delicate olive oil that won't mask the taste of the sweet lobster: one from Liguria is our first choice. Most people shudder at the thought of not boiling the lobster before pulling out its meat, but the best way to kill it is with a swift plunge with a knife into the back of the head. It's also the best way to retain the lobster's flavor, which would otherwise be lost to the boiling water. If you don't feel comfortable, ask your fishmonger to cut the lobster in half for you. We remove most of the raw meat from the shell; the hard-to-reach pieces are easier to pull out once the shell is sautéed in hot oil.

Trenette with Lobster

Trenette con Astice   *Makes 6 first-course servings*

Two 1-pound lobsters
¾ cup extra virgin olive oil
2 garlic cloves, crushed and peeled
1½ pounds tomatoes, peeled, halved, seeded, and julienned
Pinch crushed hot red pepper
Salt
1 pound trenette or fettuccine
¼ cup brandy
¼ cup dry white wine
2 tablespoons chopped flat-leaf parsley

Bring a large pot of water to a boil.

Place the lobster belly side down on a cutting board. Using a sharp, sturdy kitchen knife, split the lobster in half lengthwise. Remove the meat from the body and tail and cut into 1-inch pieces. Add to a bowl, then repeat with the other lobster. Reserve the shells.

Twist off the claws. To remove the meat, give each claw a firm blow with a flat-bottomed mallet to crack the shell. Repeated strikes should be avoided, as they will cause splintering, and shell fragments will be mixed with the meat. Using your fingers, remove the meat. Cut into 1-inch pieces and transfer to a bowl. Set aside.

Heat half the olive oil in a large saucepan over medium-high heat. Place the lobster shells, open sides down, in the pan. Cover and cook for 5 to 7 minutes. Using tongs, transfer the shells to a plate. Once cool enough to handle, transfer to the bowl. Let cool slightly. Any leftover meat can now be pulled from the shells and transferred to the bowl.

Add the remaining olive oil to the pan. Over medium heat, add the garlic, tomatoes, and crushed red pepper. Cook, stirring often, until the tomatoes soften, about 10 minutes.

Meanwhile, salt the boiling water and cook the pasta until al dente.

While the pasta cooks, add the lobster meat to the saucepan, season with salt, and cook for 1 to 2 minutes. Add the brandy and cook until it is almost completely reduced, about a minute. Add the white wine and reduce it by half. Remove and discard the garlic clove.

Drain the pasta and add it to the saucepan. Stir in the parsley, then taste for salt and add if necessary. Toss to combine and serve immediately.

Like many of da Fiore's seasonal pasta dishes, this one is an adaptation of a *secondo piatto* that Mara's grandmother used to prepare. Tiny, tender calamari are at their peak during the same few weeks in spring when sweet peas flood the market. The fusilli is Mara's innovation: corkscrew-shaped pasta captures the rich base of butter, Ligurian oil, and pancetta in the spirals. Mara adds a bit of butter when cooking peas to coax out their natural sweetness.

Fusilli with Squid and Peas

Fusilli con Calamari e Piselli   *Makes 6 first-course servings*

4 tablespoons (½ stick) unsalted butter
½ cup extra virgin olive oil
2 slices (about 2 ounces) pancetta, cut into cubes
½ small onion, sliced thin
2 garlic cloves, crushed
2 cups fresh or frozen peas
2 tablespoons chopped flat-leaf parsley
1 cinnamon stick
1 cup water
1 pound fusilli
¾ pound baby calamari (substitute large calamari),
    cleaned and cut into 2-inch segments
1 teaspoon thyme leaves
2 tablespoons dry white wine
3 tablespoons grated Parmigiano-Reggiano

Bring a large pot of water to a boil.

To prepare the sauce, melt the butter and half the olive oil in a large skillet over medium-high heat. Add the pancetta, onion, and one garlic clove, and cook until they just start to brown, 3 to 4 minutes. Add the peas, parsley, and cinnamon stick and toss or stir to combine. Cook for 2 to 3 minutes, then add a cup of water and cover. Cook until a few peas can be easily mashed between two fingers, 15 minutes; add a spoonful of water if necessary. There should be only a small amount of liquid in the pan at the completion of cooking.

Salt the boiling water and cook the pasta until tender but firm, stirring occasionally. Drain the pasta.

Meanwhile, in a medium skillet, heat the remaining oil and garlic over medium-high heat. When the garlic just starts to brown, add the calamari and thyme and season with salt and pepper. Cook, tossing or stirring, for 2 to 3 minutes, then add the white wine; cook for another minute. Mix into the saucepan with the peas and add the pasta and cheese. Toss or stir to combine, then taste for salt and add some if necessary. Serve immediately.

Acqua Alta

To KNOW THE REAL VENICE, put on your *stivali di gomma* (rubber boots) and wade through shin-high *acqua alta,* the rising tides that often roll into and over the city streets. They've always been a part of life here in Venice, and although they can signal a storm headed our way, we are never too concerned about floods. Piazza San Marco under a pool of water is such a regular sight between September and April that the city often doesn't bother to put away the elevated platforms that function as walkways. At da Fiore, we occasionally roll up our pants legs and lift the floor-length tablecloths when water rolls into the front bar area. When the tide recedes in an hour or so, the floor is mopped, the walls are dried, and we go on with our business.

Bigoli, the Veneto's traditional whole wheat or buckwheat pasta, is as popular today as ever. In the country, the thick and chewy bigoli becomes a base for hearty game sauces, but in Venice, one recipe dominates—onions and sardines, cooked down in this sweet, rustic sauce that Venetians enjoy hot or cold, any time of the year. Decades ago, a press with round openings for extruding the pasta was used to make these long strands—the process left a rough exterior, perfect for the sauce to cling to. Nowadays, most home cooks use a pasta maker or purchase the bigoli from high-quality artisanal producers. Store-bought whole-wheat spaghetti is fine, but look for those with rough edges (a sign of high-quality production).

Whole Wheat Pasta with Salsa
Bigoli in Salsa   *Makes 4 first-course servings*

Salsa
¾ pound sardines, salt-packed
1 cup dry white wine
½ cup extra virgin olive oil
3 medium onions, thinly sliced

Bigoli
3 cups whole wheat flour plus a little more for dusting
3 large eggs
⅓ cup plus 2 tablespoons water
Pinch salt

2 tablespoons chopped flat-leaf parsley

Rub the salt from the sardines. Soak for an hour in ½ cup of the white wine and enough water to cover by 3 inches. Remove the heads. In the same soaking liquid, rinse the sardines and remove the scales and backbone, separating the two fillets. Chop the fillets in pieces and set aside.

To prepare the salsa, heat the olive oil in a medium saucepan over medium-high heat. Add the onions and sardines, and cook, stirring often, until the onions begin to brown, about 10 minutes. Add the remaining white wine, letting it evaporate slightly, about a minute. Pour enough water in the pan to cover the onions. Bring to a boil, then reduce the heat and cover; cook slowly, stirring occasionally, until the onions are almost dissolved and you have a chunky sauce, about 45 minutes.

Meanwhile, to prepare the pasta, place a mound of flour on a pasta board or clean work surface. Use a fork to make a center well. Put the eggs, water, and salt in the well. With the fork, mix together the liquid, then begin incorporating the flour from the inside rim of the well. Continue to push the flour into the liquid ingredients, pulling the pieces of dough together with your hands. Scrape the board with a pastry scraper to gather all of the dough; if too dry, add another tablespoon or two of water. Knead the dough, dusting the board with flour if too moist, until you have a smooth and elastic ball of dough, about 5 minutes. Wrap the dough in plastic wrap and set aside to rest for 30 minutes.

Line a tray with clean kitchen towels. Set the pasta roller on the widest setting, and cut the pasta in two pieces. Flatten each piece of dough into a rectangle and feed it through the rollers. Repeat the process eight to nine times, folding the dough in half each time and dusting with flour to prevent sticking. Cut the pasta into 16-inch-long rectangles. Fit the pasta machine with the spaghetti attachment and pass the rectangles through. Place on the towel-lined tray until ready to use.

Fill a large pot with water and bring to a boil. Salt the boiling water and cook the bigoli until tender but firm, 8 to 9 minutes. Heat the sauce. Drain the pasta and add it to the sauce with the parsley; toss to coat and serve immediately.

MAURIZIO SUGGESTS: There's a custom of drinking a glass of water before eating *bigoli in salsa* to help with the digestion of the onions. But Mara's method of salting the onions does away with their disturbing gases, so we're free to drink dry, white sparkling wine, such as Prosecco.

Festa Della Sensa

ON THE SIXTH THURSDAY after Easter, on the sacramental holiday of Ascension, Venice celebrates one of the city's oldest festivals. Venice's metaphorical marriage to the sea first took place in a ceremony led by the doge Pietro Orseolo in A.D. 1000, after Venice conquered Dalmatia. The doge threw a ring into the ocean, and said, in effect, "We wed thee, O Sea, in a token of true and lasting dominion!" Each year, Venetians relive the ceremony as city government representatives toss a ring into the water. The rest of the city celebrates by eating bowls full of *bigoli in salsa*. Its primary ingredients, onions and sardines, are two of our region's most humble and most plentiful.

When Mara and Maurizio return from Alba with the first white truffles of autumn, it means that these pillowy, bite-size bundles of pumpkin gnocchi will be on da Fiore's menu. Slicked with sage butter and topped with just a few truffle slivers, the aroma is blissful and the taste divine.

Begin an elegant dinner party with this do-ahead dish, since these gnocchi keep for twenty-four hours uncooked in the refrigerator. Admittedly, not everyone will have a fresh truffle on hand for shaving over the top at the table. Not to worry—this dish is delicious without it.

Pumpkin Gnocchi with Parmigiano, Sage, and White Truffles

Gnocchi di Zucca con Parmigiano, Salvia, e Tartufo   *Makes 6 first-course servings*

One 2½- to 3-pound Kabocha or butternut squash, or
    pumpkin
1 cup water
1½ teaspoons salt
¼ teaspoon ground nutmeg
1½ cups all-purpose flour
1 large egg
1¾ cups grated Parmigiano-Reggiano
10 tablespoons (1¼ sticks) unsalted butter
12 sage leaves
6 ounces white truffles (optional), brushed clean

Preheat the oven to 400°F. Remove the stem, if present, from the squash or pumpkin, then slice between the vertical grooves to produce thick, half-moon slices. Scrape out and discard the seeds and strings. Place the squash on their sides in one layer on a large baking sheet. Roast until a knife easily pierces the flesh, about 25 minutes. Let cool slightly. When cool enough to handle, scrape the flesh from the skin into a sieve. Using a rubber scraper or spatula, work the squash through the sieve into a bowl. Measure 1½ cups of squash puree.

Transfer the puree to a medium saucepan and add the water, salt, and nutmeg. When it begins to boil, add a cup of the flour, a little at a time, stirring constantly. Reduce the heat to medium and cook, stirring constantly, until the mixture pulls together as a smooth, bright orange ball, about 10 minutes. Remove from the heat and beat in the egg, then 1½ cups of the cheese. Turn out onto a clean work surface and let cool slightly. When cool enough to handle, knead the remaining ½ cup flour into the

dough to form a smooth ball. Divide the dough into eight pieces and roll each into a ½-inch-thick log, dusting the work surface with flour as necessary to prevent sticking. Cut the logs into 1-inch-long segments. Spread some flour on a baking sheet, add the gnocchi, and shake to lightly coat. Set aside until ready to cook. The gnocchi can be stored, covered, and refrigerated, for up to a day.

To prepare the sauce, in a large skillet, melt the butter over medium-high heat. Add the sage and cook until it starts to crisp, 2 to 3 minutes. Set aside.

Bring a large pot of water to a boil. Salt the water and cook the gnocchi in four to five batches until they rise to the surface, about 2 minutes. Using a slotted spoon, transfer the cooked gnocchi to the skillet with the sauce. When all of the gnocchi are cooked, place the pan over high heat for 1 to 2 minutes and toss the gnocchi with the sauce. Remove from the heat, add the remaining ¼ cup Parmigiano, and toss again. Divide the gnocchi among serving plates and shave the white truffles, if using, over the top.

MAURIZIO SUGGESTS: When I think of this dish, the earthy aroma of the Piemonte comes to mind. One of its local wines, such as a not too young, ruby-red Barbera d'Asti, is a perfect match.

Truffles (*Tartufi*)

THERE'S A LITTLE REFRIGERATOR in da Fiore's kitchen that holds a small, rice-filled wooden box. Inside hides a single white truffle that's usually no larger than a small egg. When Mara reaches for this box, the kitchen staff falls silent as they watch her pull back the top and place the truffle atop a linen napkin resting on a silver platter. My father polishes the truffle shaver, and when Mara gives the cue, all eyes follow him out into the dining room. A heady aroma fills the air, and everyone watches intently as he shaves a few paper-thin slices of truffle over a plate of risotto, gnocchi, or tagliolini.

The reverence and ceremony that surrounds white truffles is not unique to Venice. These rare tubers come from the countryside around Alba, in Piemonte, where they grow underground at the roots of certain trees. Though they're much too pungent to pair with fish, they add unforgettable warmth to other seasonal ingredients on our menu, such as winter squash and mushrooms.

If you are lucky enough to buy a white truffle, look for a firm, pale specimen—a cross-section cut should display a tight, busy pattern. Bury it in a jar or box filled with rice or sea salt in the refrigerator and use it soon after you buy it.

Mara offers these ravioli, sweet with scampi and scallops, at special occasions and large parties, when cooking ahead is essential. If you decide to do the same, sprinkle the ravioli with semolina flour so they don't become gummy and stick together, and cover them with a towel and refrigerate for up to twenty-four hours. The procedure outlined below doesn't require any special tools, but you can use a ravioli mold if you have one.

For years, we served this rich ravioli in its simplest form, tossed with butter and a spoonful of fish broth. Now Mara pairs them with seasonal vegetables, such as spring peas, summer tomatoes and basil, fall's first artichoke hearts, and wintry fennel.

Seafood Ravioli with Seasonal Vegetable Sauces

Ravioli di Pesce con Sugo di Verdure di Stagione   *Makes 4 to 6 first-course servings*

Fresh Pasta
4 cups all-purpose flour
4 large eggs
¼ cup water
3 tablespoons olive oil
1½ teaspoons salt
1 egg, lightly beaten

Filling
¼ cup extra virgin olive oil
3 ounces fillet of sole, cut in small pieces
3 ounces turbot, cut in small pieces
6 ounces medium shrimp, peeled, deveined, and cut in pieces
½ tablespoon chopped basil
Salt and freshly ground black pepper
½ cup ricotta cheese
1 large egg
2 tablespoons poppy seeds

Seasonal Sauce
½ pound (2 sticks) unsalted butter
Vegetable of the season (spring: 1½ cups fresh peas; summer:
    1 cup peeled, chopped tomatoes plus 2 tablespoons chopped
    basil; fall: 4 cooked artichoke bottoms, cut in eighths;
    winter: small fennel bulb, cored and thinly sliced
3 tablespoons all-purpose flour
1 cup warm Fish Broth (page 14)
Salt

To prepare the pasta, place a mound of flour on a pasta board or clean work surface. Use a fork to make a center well. Put the eggs, water, oil, and salt in the well. With the fork, mix together the liquid, then begin incorporating the flour from the inside rim of the well. Continue to push the flour into the liquid ingredients, pulling the pieces of dough together with your hands. Scrape the board with a pastry scraper to gather all the dough. Knead the dough, dusting the board with flour if too moist, until you have a smooth, elastic ball of dough, about 10 minutes. Wrap the dough in plastic wrap and set aside to rest for 30 minutes.

To prepare the fish filling, heat the oil in a large skillet over medium-high heat. Add the sole, turbot, shrimp, and basil and season with salt and pepper. Cook, stirring often, until the fish is just cooked, about 5 minutes. Using the back of a wooden spoon, mash the fish to break it apart. Transfer to a bowl and cool quickly in an ice bath. Add the ricotta and egg and lightly beat until smooth and there are no large chunks of fish. Cover and refrigerate until ready to use. The filling can be made up to a day in advance.

Line a tray with clean kitchen towels. Set the pasta roller on the widest setting; cut the pasta in four pieces. Flatten each piece of dough into a rectangle and feed it through the rollers. Repeat the process eight to nine times, folding the dough in half each time and dusting with flour to prevent sticking. Trim the pasta sheets into long rectangles. Use a damp kitchen towel to cover the sheets that you are not working with and place a pasta sheet on a work surface with the long side facing you. Using a pastry brush, lightly brush the surface with the egg. Place dots of the filling (about 2 teaspoons) at 4-inch intervals horizontally and 2 inches vertically. The filling should not be more than 3 inches from the edges of the pasta. Take one of the horizontal side ends of the pasta and fold it over to the middle of the next row of filling, covering the first. Using a pastry cutter, cut along the line where the pasta meets, then continue advancing, folding the pasta forward over the next row of filling until you reach the end. You will have rows of filling sandwiched between sheets of pasta. Using the cutter, cut between the filling to form square ravioli. Lightly press down on the seams.

Bring a large pot of water to a boil.

To prepare the sauce, melt the butter in a medium-size skillet over medium-high heat. Add the seasonal vegetable and cook, stirring often, for about 5 minutes. Stir in the flour, making sure the mixture is smooth and there are no lumps, then add the warm fish broth. Bring to a boil, then remove from the heat. Taste for salt, adding if necessary. The sauce should coat the back of a spoon but not be too thick. Add a little warm fish broth or hot water if it is necessary to thin it.

Salt the boiling water and cook the ravioli, in batches if necessary, until tender but firm, about 2 minutes. Heat the sauce. Using a skimmer, transfer the cooked ravioli to the sauce and toss to coat. Divide among serving plates, sprinkle with poppy seeds, and serve immediately.

MAURIZIO SUGGESTS: A dry, lightly fragrant, sparkling white wine, such as Ribolla Spumante.

Risotto

ICE IS MORE THAN A STAPLE STARCH in the Veneto: it's both a showcase for seasonal ingredients and a way of drawing out their flavors. It's believed that Saracen traders introduced rice to Europe toward the end of the last millennium, but it wasn't until the fourteenth century that these pearly grains made their way to the Veneto. Venetian traders quickly determined that the low-lying area between the Po and Adige rivers was well suited to rice production. Today, the Po Valley is Europe's largest producer of rice.

The eighteen-minute miracle that transforms rice and a handful of flavorings into tender risotto is one of the most satisfying culinary exercises. The elements in your kitchen, from how well your pots retain heat to just how vigorously you're able to stir, may require more or less time. At da Fiore, Mara has risotto-making in 18 minutes down to a science.

All risotto begins with soffritto, a flavor base of aromatics cooked in fat. Unlike many cooks, Mara doesn't coat her rice in the soffritto. Instead, she adds the rice, vegetables, and the first ladleful of broth at the same time to avoid scorching the rice, so that each kernel soaks up the maximum amount of flavor. Mara uses sunflower oil to start her soffritto, since extra virgin olive oil can be too assertive.

Italian rice, generally medium- to short-grained, comes to market in three quality grades; *comune* and *fino,* the lesser two grades, are used for everything from soups to desserts. When preparing risotto, we stick to *super fino,* the highest grade.

Mara believes that Arborio, the most widely available short-grain rice in North America, isn't the best rice to use for risotto: the margin between undercooked and overcooked is too slim. Since there's not enough starch in the center of the grain, it can break down quickly, yielding a softer risotto that becomes mushy. Instead, use Vialone Nano, or even better, Carnaroli, a shorter, wider grain that Mara calls the "prince of rice." Both Vialone Nano and Carnaroli are widely available.

Risotto-making is a flexible and somewhat forgiving art, but it does require your complete attention. Vigorous stirring helps the rice's outer starch to break down into a creamy, cohesive binding liquid. This liquid is particularly important to Venetians, since we prefer a soupier risotto that's *all'onda,* or "on the wave." Mara recommends leaving your risotto alone and not stirring for a minute or two from time to time early in the process, so that the rice can absorb all of the liquid before you add the next ladleful. Any broth that's short of simmering will lower the temperature in the pot and wreak havoc on your risotto. Don't make too many portions at once: two or three for a small to medium pot, and five to six for a large one gives you room enough to stir, but not so much room that you risk scorching the rice on the bottom of the pot.

This dramatic risotto, glossy black with the stewed ink of local cuttlefish, is one of our most traditional dishes, and it never fails to raise the eyebrows of those who order it for the first time. After one bite, they're instant fans—seppia is sweeter and more tender than calamari, and its ink is far richer. The secret ingredient in this risotto is the lemon zest, which adds an aromatic lift to the seppia's briny flavor.

Venetian Black Squid Ink Risotto

Risotto con Seppie Nero ❧ *Makes 4 first-course servings*

2 cups short-grain rice, preferably Carnaroli or Vialone Nano
    rice
½ recipe Black Squid Venetian Style (page 185)
1½ quarts simmering Fish Broth (page 14) or
    Vegetable Broth (page 15)
2 tablespoons chopped flat-leaf parsley
1 tablespoon unsalted butter
Grated zest from 1 lemon

Combine the rice and squid ink in a medium saucepan. Bring to a boil, then reduce the heat to medium and cook, stirring often, until the rice absorbs most of the moisture from the squid. Add a cup of the fish broth. Cook at an aggressive boil, stirring often, for 16 to 17 minutes, adding a cup of broth at a time, as necessary; the rice should almost completely absorb the liquid between additions.

When the rice is al dente and the mixture moist but not watery, remove the pan from the heat. Stir in the parsley and butter and adjust the seasoning with salt to taste. Divide among serving plates and top with lemon zest. Serve immediately.

Squid for All Seasons

OUR LOCAL WATERS ARE PACKED with cephalopods of all kinds, and each brings its own allure to the table at different times of the year.

Calamari (squid): In spring, we look forward to the sweet baby squid known as *calamaretti*. Just over an inch long, their pinkish-white bodies are perfect for frying whole or enjoying raw. At three inches long, they are suitable for stuffing; any larger, they are grilled or sliced and used in any number of ways, in sauces or fried. We don't use the ink produced by calamari, as cuttlefish ink is much sweeter, darker, and more plentiful. In North America, calamari is available already cleaned, both fresh and frozen.

Seppia (cuttlefish): If Venice is associated with one sea creature, it is surely our beloved cuttlefish. Similar to squid, this cephalopod has a more ovoid body that opens off to the side, with just two long tentacles that outreach the other eight. The hard bone inside—known in English as the cuttlebone—is usually removed before cooking. Its tender flesh has a richer, more complex taste than squid, and we find its ink far superior.

Between July and September, we enjoy the sweet and delicate thimble-size *seppioline* fried. Later in the fall, when they're about six inches long, they're perfect for stuffing. When we cook them in their ink, we use the largest specimens, since they contain more ink. Like calamari, cuttlefish are almost always cleaned before they come to the market. If you plan on cooking with the ink, call ahead and ask your fishmonger not to clean the seppia, leaving the ink sacs intact. If you find frozen cuttlefish that still contains its ink sacs, use the meat, but not the ink—the consistency is too granular. Frozen ink with preservatives is available at specialty food stores as are the packets of liquid ink.

Polipo (octopus): *Polpetti* and *moscardini* are both tiny varieties of young octopus with tender flesh that are simply boiled and popped in the mouth. Fall is their best season.

When Mara first started preparing this risotto twenty-three years ago, Venetians weren't used to mixing seafood and vegetables in the same dish. Risottos featured either the flavors of the sea or the flavors of the earth—*basta!* Once Mara experimented with bringing the two together, it was a revelation. Radicchio in winter, asparagus in spring, zucchini in summer, and porcini in fall all get a lift from sweet scampi. If you can, purchase head-on large shrimp for an even richer broth.

Shrimp Risotto with Seasonal Flavors

Risotto con Scampi e Sapori di Stagione   *Makes 6 first-course servings*

2 pounds large shrimp, heads removed
3 quarts water
1 sprig thyme
1 bay leaf
3 to 4 black peppercorns
¾ cup mild oil, preferably sunflower
¼ small onion, diced
Seasonal vegetables (see below)
Salt
1½ pounds (3 cups) Carnaroli or Vialone Nano rice
2 tablespoons chopped flat-leaf parsley
1 tablespoon unsalted butter

Seasonal Vegetables

WINTER
2 heads radicchio di Treviso, core removed, cut crosswise into
   thin ribbons
SPRING
12 green asparagus spears, stems peeled and cut into 2-inch
   segments, tips reserved separately
SUMMER
2 medium zucchini, halved lengthwise, sliced into ¼-inch-
   thick half-moons

6 fresh porcini mushrooms, brushed clean and sliced, or ½
    ounce dried, broken in small pieces, soaked for 30 minutes,
    and drained

Peel and devein the shrimp. Set aside. Prepare a shrimp broth by placing the peels in a medium saucepan with the water, thyme, bay leaf, and peppercorns. Over medium–high heat, bring to a boil. Season with salt and reduce the heat to a simmer for 30 minutes. Strain, return to the saucepan, and place over low heat to keep hot.

In a medium heavy-bottomed saucepan, heat the oil over medium heat. Add the onion and cook, stirring, until soft, about 3 minutes. Add the vegetable of the season and cook for another 2 to 3 minutes (if using asparagus, add only the stems at this point). Add the shrimp, season with salt, and cook, stirring, until the shrimp turn pink, about 2 minutes. Stir in the rice, then add a cup of the hot shrimp broth. Cook at an aggressive boil, stirring often, for 16 to 17 minutes, adding a cup of broth at a time, as necessary; the rice should almost completely absorb the broth between additions. If using asparagus, add the tips during the last 5 minutes of cooking. When the rice is al dente and the mixture moist but not watery, remove the pan from the heat. Stir in the parsley and butter and adjust the seasoning with salt to taste. Serve immediately.

MAURIZIO SUGGESTS: The ideal wine with dishes that mix the flavors of the sea and the earth is a dry red one, such as a blend of Cabernet Franc, Sauvignon, and Merlot grapes from Veneto.

Our simplest risotto is infused with nothing more than the aromatic herbs that Mara brings back to da Fiore from our country garden. Their combined effect is hauntingly rich and surprisingly substantial. If you have to leave out one herb, another one will step up to the plate.

When making vegetable broth for this risotto, add a handful of all the herbs and let it cook down for a half hour. Discard the cooked herbs before ladling the broth into the risotto.

Risotto with Aromatic Herbs

Risotto di Erbe Aromatiche *Makes 4 first-course servings*

2 fennel bulbs with feathery fronds
Leaves from 3 rosemary sprigs
1 cup flat-leaf parsley leaves
20 basil leaves, cut into long ribbons
10 sage leaves, cut into long ribbons
1 bunch chives, snipped into ½-inch pieces
½ cup extra virgin olive oil
½ small onion, finely chopped
Salt
2 tablespoons dry white wine
2 cups Carnaroli or Vialone Nano rice
1½ quarts hot Vegetable Broth (page 15)
½ cup grated Parmigiano-Reggiano
2 tablespoons unsalted butter

Remove the fronds from the fennel stems. Roughly chop them with the rosemary and parsley leaves. Finely mince the fennel stems. Combine with the basil, sage, and chives; you should have about 1½ cups of mixed herbs.

In a medium, heavy-bottomed saucepan, heat the oil over medium heat. Add the onion and cook, stirring, until soft, about 3 minutes. Add the herbs, season with salt, and cook, stirring often, for 2 to 3 minutes. Add the white wine, cook for another minute, then stir in the rice. Add a cup of the hot vegetable broth. Cook at an aggressive boil, stirring often, for 8 minutes, adding a cup of broth at a

time, as necessary; the rice should almost completely absorb the broth between additions. Add the Parmigiano, stirring to incorporate, then continue cooking, adding broth as necessary, until the rice is al dente and the mixture moist but not watery, about 8 minutes. Remove the pan from the heat. Stir in the butter and adjust the seasoning with salt if necessary. Divide the rice among serving plates and serve immediately.

MAURIZIO SUGGESTS: A young, dry, and lightly acidic white, such as Ribolla Gialla del Friuli.

The coupling of squash and Parmigiano-Reggiano in risotto is a classic. Butternut squash is a sweeter substitution for our Mantovano squash, but if you prefer, you can use a pound of Kabocha squash, which is more savory and a bit more fibrous. Here is your opportunity to break out that bottle of aged Balsamico Tradizionale that you bought in Italy—a sweet-sour drizzle of it bolsters these creamy flavors. The longer it's aged, the more syrupy the consistency will be and the better it will taste over this risotto.

Butternut Squash Risotto Drizzled with Aged Balsamic Vinegar

Risotto di Zucca e Parmigiano con Aceto Balsamico   *Makes 6 first-course servings*

1 small butternut squash or 1 Kabocha squash (about 1 pound)
¾ cup mild oil, preferably sunflower oil
¼ small onion, diced
Salt
1½ pounds (3 cups) Carnaroli or Vialone Nano rice
2 quarts hot Vegetable Broth (page 15)
1 cup grated Parmigiano-Reggiano
1 tablespoon unsalted butter
Aged balsamic vinegar for drizzling

Trim the ends from the butternut squash. Using a vegetable peeler, remove the skin. Cut the squash in half lengthwise and scoop out the seeds and fibers. Divide each squash half in quarters. Using a knife or mandoline on a fine slicing setting, cut the squash pieces into ⅛-inch-thick slices.

In a medium, heavy-bottomed saucepan, heat the oil over medium heat. Add the onion and cook, stirring, until soft, about 3 minutes. Add the butternut squash, season with salt, and cover with water. Cook, simmering, until the squash easily breaks apart, about 20 minutes. Stir in the rice, then add a cup of the hot vegetable broth. Cook at an aggressive boil, stirring often, for 8 minutes, adding a cup of broth at a time, as necessary; the rice should almost completely absorb the broth between additions. Add the Parmigiano, stirring to incorporate, then continue cooking, adding broth as necessary, until the rice is al dente and the mixture moist but not watery, about 8 minutes. Remove the pan from the heat. Stir in the butter and adjust the seasoning with salt if necessary. Divide the rice among serving plates and drizzle with balsamic vinegar. Serve immediately.

Zuppe

A GOOD SOUP IS PERHAPS THE MOST SATISFYING OF ALL DISHES, ELEVAT-ING HUMBLE INGREDIENTS LIKE NO OTHER RECIPE. POTATOES, WHICH Mara uses to thicken most of her soups, impart a rich, velvety texture and weight without any additional fat. Onions also play an important role in most of our soups, although their flavor isn't as assertive as you would expect, because Mara first salts them, like eggplant. She thinly slices the onions, covers them generously with fine sea salt, and lets them drain in a colander for two hours to release their gases and drain the acidity that causes upset stomachs and irritability in many people. Then she rinses them under a steady stream of cold water for a good long while to remove as much salt as possible. Taste them—they'll be somewhat salty, and quite sweet, so there's no need to add additional salt to your soup.

When green peas were first brought to Venice during the Renaissance, they were as prized and as rare as truffles. *Risi e bisi,* a rice and pea risotto in a luxurious broth made from the shells and shoots, flecked with pancetta and parsley and perfumed with cinnamon, was served to the doge annually on April 25, Venice's feast day, called La Festa di San Marco.

It's no coincidence that peas are at their peak of flavor on this day every year. The best still come from the lagoon near Chioggia and Sant' Erasmo, although for this recipe, even frozen peas will work. Because we love the luxurious broth so much, Venetians prefer to prepare this like a soup, so it's the only risotto we serve with a spoon!

Rice and Peas

Risi e Bisi   *Makes 6 servings*

2½ pounds fresh peas in their pods
3 quarts water
Salt
3 tablespoons unsalted butter
2 tablespoons olive or sunflower oil
2 ounces pancetta, diced
1 small yellow onion, minced
½ cinnamon stick
1½ pounds (3 cups) Carnaroli or Vialone Nano rice
½ bunch flat-leaf parsley leaves, minced
⅓ cup freshly grated Parmigiano-Reggiano plus
    some for sprinkling
Freshly ground black pepper

Shell the peas, reserving the pods. Place the pods in a medium pot with 3 quarts lightly salted water. Bring to a boil over high heat, reduce the heat to medium-low, and simmer, uncovered, for an hour. Strain the broth into a medium pot, pressing on the pods. Discard the pods. Keep the broth warm over medium heat.

Melt a tablespoon of the butter and the oil in a large, heavy pot over medium heat. Add the pancetta and onion and cook, stirring until the onion is golden, about 10 minutes. Add the peas, cinnamon stick, and ½ cup of the broth. Cover and cook until the peas are tender, about 5 minutes.

Increase the heat to high, uncover, and cook off any remaining liquid. Add the rice and stir to coat well. Add about ¾ cup warm broth and cook, stirring constantly, until most of the broth has been absorbed. Add about ¾ cup more broth. Continue cooking, stirring and adding broth as needed, until the rice is tender but firm to the bite, about 18 minutes. Remove from the heat and stir in just enough broth so that the rice is loose but not watery, about a cup (*risi e bisi* should be slightly soupier than ordinary risotto). Stir in the remaining 2 tablespoons butter, the parsley, and the ⅓ cup Parmigiano. Cover and allow to rest for a few minutes. Serve with additional Parmigiano-Reggiano and sprinkle with black pepper.

From Trieste to Chioggia to our very own Venezia, every cook in every town along the Adriatic coast makes his or her own version of this traditional, one-pot seafood stew. This brodetto, called *broeto* in Venetian dialect, is true to its centuries-old tradition: its mild broth, laced with a touch of thyme and fresh vegetables, accentuates the flavors of the fish without any of the heavy seasonings characteristic of other Mediterranean fish stews, such as *ciuppin* and *burrida* from Liguria, *cacciucco* from Tuscany and, of course, *bouillabaisse* from France.

Although the ingredient list is long, the recipe is simple. Exact portioning and mandatory ingredients violate the soulful spirit of *brodetto;* if you can't find all the types of fish listed here, feel free to give and take. Just make sure that the total weight of the fish adds up.

Brodetto can be enjoyed immediately, but it's better the next day. Sprinkle it with some fresh basil leaves (torn with your hands, not cut with a knife) just before serving. Don't wait much longer than twenty-four hours to enjoy *brodetto,* though, since the flavor of the soup grows stronger as it sits, and the fish will fall apart.

Venetian Seafood Stew

***Brodetto di Pesce* alla Veneziana**   *Makes 6 servings*

8 ounces mussels, beards removed, scrubbed and well rinsed

8 ounces clams, scrubbed and well rinsed

¾ cup extra virgin olive oil

2 celery stalks, finely chopped

1 carrot, peeled and finely chopped

¼ onion, finely chopped

2 garlic cloves, crushed

Leaves from 3 sprigs thyme

1 medium tomato, peeled, seeded, and chopped

8 ounces baby calamari, cleaned
   (If you can find only large calamari, cut them in half)

8 ounces medium shrimp, peeled and deveined

3 ounces red mullet fillet, cut into 1-inch pieces

3 ounces sole fillet, cut into 1-inch pieces

3 ounces halibut fillet, cut into 1-inch pieces

3 ounces monkfish fillet, cut into 1-inch pieces

3 large scallops, halved crosswise

1 cup dry white wine
2 quarts simmering Fish Broth (page 14)

Place the mussels and clams in a medium saucepan. Add a cup of water, cover, and cook over medium-high heat until the shells are open, about 6 minutes. Discard any unopened shells. Let cool slightly, then remove the meat from the clams and mussels. Set aside. Reserve the cooking liquid.

In a large saucepan or braising pan, heat the oil over medium-low heat. Add the celery, carrot, onion, garlic, and thyme and cook, stirring often, for 10 minutes; do not allow the vegetables to brown. Add the tomato and cook for another 5 minutes. Remove and discard the garlic cloves.

Add the baby calamari and cook, stirring here and there, for 2 minutes. Add the shrimp; cook for a minute. Season the red mullet, sole, halibut, and monkfish with salt. Add them to the pan along with the scallops. Gently move the fish around the pan to cook evenly. After 2 to 3 minutes, add the white wine and cook until it evaporates by half. Add the reserved liquid from the clams and mussels; leave behind the bottom quarter of the liquid, which will likely contain sand. Using a ladle, spoon in the simmering fish broth. Immediately remove the pan from the heat. Adjust the seasoning to taste and serve immediately, or cool quickly in an ice bath and serve, reheated, the next day.

The lowly bean holds a privileged rank at the Venetian table, thanks to local specimens such as the *Borlotti* and *Lamon* that were introduced to the northern province of Belluno, near the Dolomite Mountains, in the sixteenth century. Their mottled skins (*Lamon* are red and white, *Borlotti*, red and brown) are thin and tender, contributing to a beautifully textured soup. Mara adds small clams just before serving to impart a new dimension to this classic recipe. The younger the dried beans, the better the soup. Look for beans that are less than a year old at specialty food markets.

The flavor of this soup only improves with time. Let it rest for at least twenty-four hours in the refrigerator, then reheat. Top with croutons, drizzle with olive oil (preferably a peppery Tuscan one), and ladle the clams and their liquor over the top.

Bean Soup with Clams

Zuppa di Fagioli con Vongole   *Makes 4 to 6 servings*

1 pound dried borlotti beans
3 quarts water
¼ cup plus 2 tablespoons olive oil
1 celery stalk, chopped
1 medium carrot, peeled and chopped
½ medium onion, chopped
2 garlic cloves, crushed
1 medium tomato, diced
1 sprig rosemary
Salt
1½ pounds clams, well rinsed
¼ cup dry white wine
2 tablespoons chopped flat-leaf parsley
1 cup unseasoned croutons or 6 crostini

Rinse the beans, picking out any pebbles or shriveled beans, then place in a bowl and add the water; soak overnight.

Heat the ¼ cup oil in a medium saucepan set over medium heat. Add the celery, carrot, onion, and 1 clove garlic and cook, stirring often, until the vegetables soften, about 5 minutes. Remove and discard the garlic. Add the beans and their soaking liquid, the tomato, and rosemary. Bring to a boil, then reduce the heat and simmer uncovered until a bean can be easily mashed, about 2 hours. Halfway through the cooking, season the soup mixture with salt.

Using a slotted spoon, remove a quarter of the bean mixture, transfer to a large bowl, and set aside. Working over the bowl, pass the remaining beans and their liquid through a medium sieve or China cap; use a stiff rubber spatula to work the soup through. Rinse the saucepan, add the contents of the bowl, and bring to a simmer over medium-low heat.

Meanwhile, to prepare the clams, heat the remaining oil and garlic in a large skillet set over medium-high heat. When the garlic just starts to brown around the edges, add the clams and white wine. Cover and cook until the clams open, 4 to 5 minutes. Discard any clams that do not open. Add the parsley and toss to combine. When the clams are cool enough to handle, pull the meat from the shells; reserve the cooking liquid.

Adjust the seasoning of the soup with salt, if necessary, then divide among the serving bowls. Place a small mound of warm clams and a spoonful of their cooking liquid in the center. Drizzle with olive oil and serve immediately with warm croutons.

Vongole (Clams)

MANY VARIETIES OF CLAMS come from the Venetian lagoon, but *veraci,* or real ones, are the most prized. Their oval shells, marked by two protruding blowholes that flush out impurities inside the shell, hide briny, tender flesh. The waters around Malamocco and Chioggia were once full of these prized clams but sadly, the clam beds are not as healthy as they once were, and *vongole veraci* are becoming a rarity. The common local clams, *bevarasse,* are larger and brinier. All recipes that call for *vongole veraci* can substitute small littlenecks, cherrystones, or manila clams. When cooking with clams, a robust olive oil from Puglia will temper their saltiness.

This eye-popping soup is as green as grass and studded with pink slivers of shrimp. Many of our American guests are surprised to learn that Italian country cooks use nettles, a wild herb that many people brush off as a nuisance. They grow like weeds and have fuzzy "stingers" in the Veneto as well, but when the leaves are cooked, they lose their sting and develop a deep, rich taste. Look for nettles in specialty food stores and at farmers' markets across North America in the summer. A light, Ligurian oil complements their herbaceous flavor.

Wild Nettle and Imperial Shrimp Soup

Zuppa di Ortiche e Mazzancolle 🐚 *Makes 4 to 6 servings*

1 small onion (about 3 ounces)
2 tablespoons coarse salt
¾ pound baby nettles
¾ pound imperial or large shrimp, peeled and deveined
4 tablespoons (½ stick) unsalted butter
3 medium potatoes (about 1 pound), peeled and cubed
6 cups water
Salt and freshly ground black pepper
3 tablespoons extra virgin olive oil plus more for drizzling
1 garlic clove, crushed
Leaves from 1 sprig thyme
2 tablespoons dry white wine
1 cup unseasoned croutons or 6 crostini

Peel and thinly slice the onion; a mandoline on its finest setting will produce uniform, thin slices. Spread the slices in a colander and evenly sprinkle the salt over the top; use your hands to mix. Set aside for 2 hours.

Thoroughly rinse the onion, squeeze out any excess water, then pat dry with a clean kitchen towel or between sheets of paper towels.

Meanwhile, clean the wild nettles, removing the leaves and discarding the stems; wear rubber gloves, as nettles have little stingers or hairs that become "deactivated" once cooked. Set aside.

Slice each shrimp in three pieces on the bias. Set aside.

Heat the butter in a medium saucepan set over medium heat. Add the onion and cook, stirring often, about 5 minutes. Add the nettle leaves and potatoes and cook for another 5 minutes. Add the water. Bring to a boil, then reduce the heat and simmer uncovered for an hour.

Puree the soup in batches in a food processor or blender. Season with salt. Set aside.

Heat the 3 tablespoons oil and the garlic in a medium skillet over medium-high heat. When the garlic browns around the edges, remove and discard it. Add the shrimp and thyme and season with salt and pepper. Cook until the shrimp turns pink, 1 to 2 minutes, then add the white wine and cook for another minute. Stir the shrimp into the soup. Divide among serving bowls, drizzle with olive oil, and serve immediately, topped with a handful of croutons or 1 crostini per bowl.

Venetian Shrimp

CRUSTACEANS OF ALL KINDS prosper in the chilly, shallow waters of the Venetian lagoon. The smallest, sweetest shrimp are literally at the bottom of the food chain, and since the larger fish eat them, they're partly responsible for Venetian seafood's sweet reputation.

Scampi: These diminutive relatives of the lobster are a staple of Venetian cooking. Known in other parts of the world as Dublin Bay prawns, langoustines, or Norway shrimp, they're actually not shrimp at all. Nor do they have anything in common with the jumbo shrimp-and-garlic preparation popularized by Italian-American restaurants. Their flesh, especially the prized tail meat, is extremely sweet and tender. In Venice they're tossed into pastas, pureed into soups, fried, or simply grilled or boiled.

Canoce (mantis shrimp): These grayish-white crustaceans, with their characteristic red spots fanning out over their tails, burrow in the mud of the lagoon during the day, and when they rise up at night, their phosphorous shells glimmering in the moonlight, Venetian fisherman are ready with nets to catch them. They're also called *cicale di mare,* named for the cricket-like sound they make in the water. The meat of the long, white body, which can range between two and five inches, is very rich and faintly sweet—a bit like lobster. Abundant year-round, they're at their best in the winter. Traditional recipes call for boiling or grilling, but Mara also purees them in soups.

Gamberetti (small shrimp): These tiny, pink sweet shrimp are a specialty of the Venetian lagoon, available in the late autumn through the early spring.

Mazzancolle (imperial shrimp): These reddish brown crustaceans are in the same family as scampi but are larger and have a more pronounced flavor. They are often grilled, or boiled and pureed to lend their briny taste to soups. Large shrimp are the best substitute, though imperial shrimp may be found at Asian markets.

Schie: These minuscule brown shrimp, just a quarter inch long, are unique to our lagoon. The sweet flesh doesn't turn pink with cooking, and they're often served simply sautéed with olive oil, garlic, and parsley alongside polenta. They're abundant in the lagoon when the water is cold. The best substitute is the tiny titi shrimp imported from Indonesia.

Our most decadent summer soup reconciles opposites—hot and cold, salty and sweet, and soft and chewy—with each luscious bite. A mound of warm oysters sits in a pool of cool mint soup, while the herb's flavor, which can assert itself a little too loudly, is tempered with sweet zucchini and young green beans. The potatoes thicken the soup.

Chilled Mint Soup with Sautéed Oysters

Zuppa Fredda di Menta con Ostriche   *Makes 4 to 6 servings*

1 medium onion (about 5 ounces)

2 tablespoons coarse salt

4 tablespoons ($\frac{1}{2}$ stick) unsalted butter

$\frac{3}{4}$ pound zucchini, sliced

3 medium potatoes (about 1 pound), peeled and cubed

$3\frac{1}{2}$ cups mint leaves

6 cups water

Salt and freshly ground black pepper

5 ounces haricots verts

30 oysters, shucked and liquid reserved

$\frac{1}{4}$ cup extra virgin olive oil plus more for drizzling

$1\frac{1}{2}$ tablespoons chives snipped into $\frac{1}{2}$-inch pieces

1 tablespoon chopped flat-leaf parsley

1 cup unseasoned croutons or 6 crostini

Peel and thinly slice the onion; a mandoline on its finest setting will produce uniform, thin slices. Spread the slices in a colander and evenly sprinkle the salt over the top; use your hands to mix. Set aside for 2 hours.

Thoroughly rinse the onion, squeeze out any excess water, then pat dry with a clean kitchen towel or between sheets of paper towels.

Melt the butter in a medium saucepan set over medium heat. When bubbly, add the onion and cook, stirring often, about 5 minutes. Add the zucchini and potatoes and cook for another 2 to 3 minutes. Stir in the mint, cook for a minute, then add the water. Bring to a boil, then reduce the heat and simmer for an hour.

Puree the soup in batches in a food processor or blender. Strain through a medium sieve into a bowl, using a rubber spatula to work the soup through. Cover and chill.

Twenty minutes before you are ready to serve the soup, bring a medium pot of water to a boil. Season with salt and add the beans. Cook until tender but firm, 3 to 4 minutes, then drain and transfer to a bowl of ice water. Drain again. Cut the beans into 2-inch segments on the bias. Set aside.

Use an oyster knife or strong dull knife to open the oysters; reserve their liquid.

Heat the ¼ cup oil in a medium skillet set over medium-high heat. Add the oysters and their liquid, the beans, chives, and parsley and season with salt and pepper. Cook, tossing or gently stirring, until the oysters are just cooked, 1 to 2 minutes.

Divide the soup among serving bowls. Place a small mound of the oyster mixture in the center. Drizzle with olive oil and top with a handful of croutons or 1 crostini per bowl.

What an elegant soup to prepare for a special gathering! Mara often cooks a batch for large dinner parties and serves little cups of it as a rich *benvenuto a tavola,* or a welcome to the table. The flavor of fresh thyme and sweet shrimp is delicate but declarative, thanks to the quick-and-easy broth prepared with the shrimp shells. We call this a consommé because the flavors are so concentrated, but since the broth is thickened with bread, it is not a traditional, clear consommé at all. Mazzancolle, or imperial shrimp, are difficult to find in North America; substitute large shrimp.

Imperial Shrimp Consommé Perfumed with Thyme

Consommé di Mazzancolle al Profumo di Timo   *Makes 6 servings*

1½ pounds large shrimp, with their shells, heads on
4 tablespoons (½ stick) unsalted butter
2 tablespoons extra virgin olive oil
2 celery stalks, diced
1 small carrot, diced
1 small onion, diced
1 garlic clove
2 sprigs thyme plus 2 teaspoons thyme leaves
⅓ cup dry white wine
6 cups water
2 slices white bread (about 2 ounces), crusts removed
1 cup unseasoned croutons or 6 crostini

Peel and devein a third of the shrimp. Cut into ½-inch pieces. Set aside.

In a medium saucepan over low heat, melt the butter in the oil. Add the celery, carrot, onion, garlic, and thyme sprigs and cook, stirring occasionally, until the vegetables soften, about 10 minutes. Remove and discard the garlic. Add the remaining shrimp, still unpeeled, increase the heat to medium-high, and cook until they become pink, 5 minutes. Add the white wine and boil until it reduces to 2 to 3 tablespoons. Add the water, bring to a boil, then reduce the heat to a simmer. Add the pieces of bread and cook, stirring to break them apart, for another 30 minutes.

Using an immersion blender or a food processor, puree the soup. Transfer to a medium sieve or China cap placed over a large bowl. Using a rubber spatula, work the soup through the sieve until smooth and velvety. Rinse the saucepan and return the pureed soup to the pan. Heat to a simmer, add the cut, peeled shrimp, then remove from the heat. Garnish with croutons and fresh thyme leaves.

These sweet and meaty local shrimp take on an earthy edge, thanks to the silvery stalks of cardoons, whose flavor resembles that of their ancient ancestor, the artichoke. This soup is at its best in November, when cardoons first arrive at the market, and the *canoce* are plump with roe and intensely sweet. Cardoons are cultivated in California and are available at specialty food stores and farmers' markets throughout the winter. Large shrimp are a fine substitute for *canoce*.

Cardoon Soup with Mantis Shrimp

Zuppa di Cardi con Canoce   *Makes 4 servings*

¾ pound Spanish onion, thinly sliced
¼ cup coarse salt
1 bunch cardoons (about 1½ pounds)
Juice of ½ lemon
16 large shrimp, peeled and deveined
¼ pound (1 stick) plus 2 tablespoons unsalted butter
¾ pound potatoes (about 2 medium), peeled and cubed
7 cups water
Salt and freshly ground black pepper

Peel and thinly slice the onion; a mandoline on its finest setting will produce uniform, thin slices. Spread the slices in a colander and evenly sprinkle the salt over the top; use your hands to mix. Set aside for 2 hours.

Meanwhile, remove any tough outer ribs from the cardoons. Trim the ends off the stalks. Using a knife, cut all leaves from the stalks (the ribs or stems are the only part that will be used). Using a vegetable peeler, peel the stalks to remove any tough fibers or filaments. Cut the inner heart and stalks into 3-inch segments. Transfer to a bowl, cover with water, and add the lemon juice to prevent browning.

Thoroughly rinse the onion, squeeze out any excess water, then pat dry with a clean kitchen towel or between sheets of paper towels. Drain the cardoons.

Slice half the shrimp in half lengthwise.

Melt the ¼ pound butter over medium-low heat in a medium saucepan. When bubbling, add the onion, increase the heat to medium–high, and cook, stirring often, for 2 to 3 minutes. Add the potatoes and cardoons, and cook for another 2 to 3 minutes. Add the water and the halved shrimp and bring the mixture to a boil. Reduce the heat and simmer until the cardoons easily break apart, about 1½ hours. Transfer the soup to a bain marie or large bowl and place in an ice bath to cool.

Puree the slightly chilled soup in batches in a food processor or in a blender. Transfer the puree to a medium sieve or China cap and, using a wooden spoon or rubber spatula, work the soup through into a clean medium saucepan. Work through as much of the solids as possible. Heat to a simmer. Adjust the seasoning with salt, if necessary; it will likely require little, if any, because of the earlier salt processing of the onions. At this point, the soup may be stored, refrigerated, in a covered container for up to 2 days.

Prepare the garnish, heating the 2 tablespoons butter in a medium skillet over medium-high heat. When bubbly, add the remaining shrimp, season with salt and pepper, and cook, tossing or stirring until they lightly brown, about 2 minutes. Divide the soup among serving bowls and top each portion with two shrimp. Serve immediately.

When the weather starts to cool down, this is one of our first cravings: Mara's hearty porcini-onion soup, thickened with potatoes and flavored with beer. We use fresh porcini when available, but dried ones yield a rich, flavorful broth. The cultivated white button mushrooms sold in supermarkets are a different *funghi* entirely and don't have enough flavor to carry this soup. Like most soups, this one is best after it has rested in the refrigerator for twenty-four hours. Simply garnish with homemade crostini before serving.

Porcini Mushroom and Onion Soup

Zuppa di Funghi Porcini e Cipolle   *Makes 4 to 6 servings*

¾ pound fresh or 1 ounce dried porcini mushrooms
1¾ pounds onions (about 2 large)
⅓ cup coarse salt
2 tablespoons olive oil
1 garlic clove, halved
Salt and freshly ground black pepper
1 cup blond beer
2 tablespoons chopped flat-leaf parsley
6 tablespoons (¾ stick) unsalted butter
2 medium potatoes, peeled and cubed
6 cups chicken or beef broth or water
3 tablespoons toasted, unseasoned breadcrumbs (see page 32)

If using dried mushrooms, place them in a bowl and cover with 3 inches water. Set aside for 2 hours.

Peel and thinly slice the onions; a mandoline on its finest setting will produce uniform, thin slices. Spread the slices in a colander and evenly sprinkle the salt over the top; use your hands to mix. Set aside for 2 hours. Rinse the onions thoroughly, squeeze out excess water, then pat dry with a clean kitchen towel or between sheets of paper towels.

If using dried porcini, lift them from their soaking liquid to a strainer or colander. Do not pour the mushrooms and liquid through a strainer, as this will distribute any dirt or grit settled at the bottom of the bowl. Reserve the soaking liquid. Rinse the porcini, then squeeze out any excess liquid; pat dry. If using fresh porcini, brush clean and slice.

In a medium skillet, heat the oil and garlic over medium-high heat. When the garlic halves begin to brown, remove and discard. Add the mushrooms, season with salt and pepper, and cook, stirring often, until the mushrooms lightly brown, about 5 minutes. Add the beer and boil to evaporate slightly, about 2 minutes. Add the parsley and cook for another minute. Using a small ladle, remove a cup of the reserved mushroom soaking liquid from the top of the bowl and add it to the skillet (use water if using fresh porcini). Take care not to disrupt the sediment at the bottom of the bowl. Simmer for 2 to 3 minutes, then remove from the heat and set aside.

In a medium saucepan, melt the butter over medium heat. Add the onions, increase the heat to medium-high, and cook, stirring often, for 2 to 3 minutes. Add the potatoes, cook for another 2 to 3 minutes, then stir in the mushrooms and their juice. Cook, stirring frequently, for 3 to 4 minutes to blend flavors, then add the broth or water. Bring the mixture to a boil, then reduce the heat and simmer for an hour; the mushrooms, onions, and potatoes should be quite soft. Let cool slightly.

Transfer the soup in batches to a food processor. Pulse eight to ten times to puree, leaving small visible bits of mushrooms. Rinse the saucepan, then return the soup to the pan. Heat to a simmer. Adjust the seasoning with salt, if necessary; it will likely require little, if any, because of the salted onions. Divide among warmed soup bowls, top with the breadcrumbs, and serve immediately.

MAURIZIO SUGGESTS: Beer or a light red wine such as a Merlot from the Veneto.

This silky, bright green local asparagus soup tastes like the essence of spring. With the first tender shoots of the season, there's no need to mix their sublime flavor with other spices or seasonings. A few potatoes for thickening, croutons for texture, and drizzles of peppery Tuscan oil are the only embellishments the soup needs.

Spring Asparagus Soup

Zuppa di Asparagi Verdi *Makes 4 to 6 servings*

¾ pound Spanish onion
¼ cup coarse salt
2 bunches asparagus (about 1¾ pounds)
6 tablespoons (¾ stick) butter
3 medium potatoes (about 1 pound), peeled and cubed
7 cups water
Salt and freshly ground black pepper
Extra virgin olive oil
1 cup unseasoned croutons or 6 crostini

Peel and thinly slice the onion; a mandoline on its finest setting will produce uniform, thin slices. Spread the slices in a colander and evenly sprinkle the salt over the top; use your hands to mix. Set aside for 2 hours.

Snap off the ends of the asparagus spears at the point where they naturally break. Cut off the tips, then slice them in half on the bias. Using a vegetable peeler, peel the stems and cut into 2-inch segments. Reserve the tips and stems separately.

Thoroughly rinse the onion, squeeze out any excess water, then pat dry with a clean kitchen towel or between sheets of paper towels.

Melt 4 tablespoons of the butter in a medium saucepan set over medium heat. Add the onions, increase the heat to medium-high, and cook, stirring often, until fragrant and soft, about 5 minutes. Add the asparagus stems and three-quarters of the tips and cook for 2 to 3 minutes. Stir in the potatoes, cook for another 2 to 3 minutes, then add the water. Bring to a boil, then reduce the heat and simmer for an hour—the asparagus should be easily crushed.

Puree the soup in batches in a food processor or blender. Strain through a medium sieve or China cap into a clean medium saucepan, using a rubber spatula to work the soup through. Bring the soup to a simmer and season to taste with salt.

Meanwhile, heat the remaining butter in a medium-size skillet over medium heat. Add the reserved asparagus tips and 1 to 2 tablespoons water and season with salt and pepper. Cook, tossing or stirring, until soft but still firm, 3 to 4 minutes.

Divide the soup among soup bowls and top with the cooked asparagus tips. Drizzle the soup with olive oil. Garnish each serving with a handful of croutons or 1 crostini and serve immediately.

MAURIZIO SUGGESTS: A dry white wine that's lightly fruity and has a balanced acidity, such as a Pinot Bianco.

Asparagus

NOTHING SIGNALS SPRING in Venice more than the bright green bunches of asparagus stacked high at the Rialto market. The lagoon's sandy soil suits asparagus well, so it grows in abundance on our market islands. At da Fiore, we often serve the thin *asparagi verdi* as an accompaniment to fish. Mara uses the more pronounced flavor of the larger, chubbier stalks for soups and risottos. The wild asparagus that grows across the countryside is a rarified treat that we feature prominently on our menu whenever we can find it.

The farmers in Bassano del Grappa, a picturesque town along the Brenta River, cover their asparagus shoots before they have a chance to poke out of the ground. Since the stalks never see the light of day, they don't produce the chlorophyll that gives asparagus its characteristic green color. The famed white stalks are wider and fleshier and their taste a bit more refined.

Our craving for this refreshing summer soup strikes at just the right time each year. When the first summer heat spell sweeps over our garden, we inevitably have more basil and zucchini than we know what to do with! The smaller, dark green zucchini that measure no more than six inches long are sweetest, and their tender texture creates a velvety soup. Immediately before serving, drizzle a thread of Tuscan olive oil over the top. The soup is just as delicious cold as it is warm.

Zucchini and Basil Soup

Vellutata di Zucchini e Basilico   *Makes 4 to 6 servings*

1 medium Spanish onion (about 5 ounces)
2 tablespoons coarse salt
¼ pound (½ stick) unsalted butter
2 pounds zucchini, sliced crosswise
3 medium potatoes (about 1 pound), peeled and cubed
7 cups water
½ cup basil cut into thin ribbons
1 cup unseasoned croutons or 6 crostini

Peel and thinly slice the onion; a mandoline on its finest setting will produce uniform, thin slices. Spread the slices in a colander and evenly sprinkle the salt over the top; use your hands to mix. Set aside for 2 hours.

Thoroughly rinse the onion, squeeze out any excess water, then pat dry with a clean kitchen towel or between sheets of paper towels.

Melt the butter in a medium saucepan set over medium heat. Add the onion, increase the heat to medium–high, and cook, stirring often, for 5 minutes. Add the zucchini and cook, stirring often, until slightly softened, about 5 minutes. Add the potatoes and cook for 2 to 3 minutes. Pour the water into the saucepan. Bring to a boil, then reduce the heat and simmer for an hour. Remove from the heat and stir in the basil.

Puree the soup in batches in a food processor or blender. Adjust the seasoning with salt, if necessary. Serve warm or chilled, garnished with a handful of croutons or 1 crostini for each serving.

Secondi Piatti

IN TRADITIONAL VENETIAN TERMS, THE SECONDO PIATTO OR "SECOND PLATE" IS THE PINNACLE OF THE MEAL, THE MAIN FISH COURSE THAT EVERY prior bite has prepared you for. Simple fish dishes such as *branzino* layered in lemons and rosemary and baked in a salt crust, or *rombo* covered with paper-thin slices of potatoes and roasted until crisp and golden, exemplify the age-old Venetian maxim that less is more. The fish's flavor takes center stage.

When da Fiore first opened in the late seventies, Venetians were still dining in restaurants as they did at home. For the secondi piatti, Mara prepared simple, whole grilled fish with vegetables on the side. She introduced fish fillets to da Fiore's menu a few years later, and our local vegetables gradually started to work their way into these main courses, adding delicate flavor, texture, or contrast. Today, we don't serve many *contorni* (side dishes) in the restaurant, since most of Mara's *secondi* recipes integrate them into each dish.

Simplicity is best when it comes to the rich, nutlike flavor of San Pietro (also known as John Dory), whose symmetrical cheek markings are believed to be the fingerprints of the saint himself. The thick, white-flaked fillets hold together well when cooked. Pan-fried in butter, they develop an even richer taste, which Mara brightens with the sweet acidity of pink grapefruit. We alternate between bites of sweet grapes and *cipollini*, the tiny, flat yellow onions. Serve with baked rice (page 17).

Fillet of John Dory with Pink Grapefruit

Filetto di San Pietro al Pompelmo Rosa   *Makes 4 servings*

4 cipollini onions
4 pink grapefruit
Four 6-ounce John Dory fillets
Salt
½ cup all-purpose flour
6 tablespoons (¾ stick) unsalted butter
Pinch ground nutmeg
Freshly ground black pepper
1 cup halved seedless red grapes
2 tablespoons snipped chives

Trim off the dark green part of the onion, leaving only the light green portion and the bulb. Cook in a large pot of boiling water until a sharp knife easily pierces the bulb, 8 to 10 minutes. Drain and cool. Cut off the root end and peel. Set aside.

Using a sharp paring knife, peel strips of the skin from two of the pink grapefruit; take care to remove only the zest (colored skin), leaving behind the bitter white pith. Cut these strips into julienne (long, thin strips). Transfer to a small saucepan and cover with a couple of inches of water. Bring to a boil and cook for 1 to 2 minutes. Drain and reserve. Squeeze the juice from all of the grapefruit. Set aside.

Season the John Dory fillets with salt and dredge in the flour, shaking off any excess. In a large skillet set over medium heat, melt the butter. When bubbly and foamy, add the fillets. Cook until lightly browned on both sides, about 2 minutes per side, then pour off any excess fat in the pan. Add the grapefruit juice and blanched zest, cipollini, and nutmeg, and season with pepper. Cook at a moderate boil until the pan juices reduce slightly, about 4 minutes. Add the grapes and chives and cook for another 30 seconds. Place a John Dory fillet and cipollini on each serving plate and spoon the pan sauce over the top. Serve immediately.

MAURIZIO SUGGESTS: A dry white wine that's not too fruity and has a good alcoholic kick, such as Malvasia del Carso.

Mara forgoes her usual restraint in seasoning fish with this lusty, southern Italian–inspired recipe. Monkfish fillets are white, meaty, and strongly flavored, and stand up to the strong, earthy flavors of the Mediterranean—ripe tomatoes, onions, olives, and capers.

You can use large, fleshy black olives, but Mara prefers the tiny gray-black Taggiasca olives from Liguria. Add the tomatoes as the last step, so that they don't color the pristine white fillets.

Mediterranean-Style Monkfish Fillets

Coda di Rospo alla Mediterranea 🐚 *Makes 4 servings*

Monkfish Broth
1 pound head and bones from monkfish, well rinsed
1 celery stalk, halved, with leafy fronds
1 carrot, quartered
½ small onion
2 sprigs thyme
3 peppercorns
2 quarts water
Salt

Monkfish
2 tablespoons extra virgin olive oil
1 garlic clove
Four 6- to 7-ounce fillets monkfish
Salt
½ cup dry white wine
1 medium tomato (about 5 ounces), peeled, seeded, and diced
8 basil leaves, cut into long ribbons
2 tablespoons capers, rinsed
¼ cup chopped black olives

1 recipe baked rice (page 17) (substitute Monkfish Broth for
   Fish Broth)

To prepare the broth, place the fish head and bones, celery, carrot, onion, thyme, and peppercorns in a large pot. Cover with the water, and season with salt. Bring to a boil, then reduce the heat and simmer for 30 minutes, skimming the surface frequently to remove the foamy scum or impurities. If using immediately, ladle the broth from the pot into the rice. Otherwise, strain the stock through a fine-mesh strainer into a container. Cool in an ice bath, then cover and refrigerate for up to 2 days.

Prepare the baked rice.

While the rice cooks, prepare the fish. Heat the oil and garlic in a large skillet over medium-high heat. Season the fillets with salt and add them to the skillet. Cook, lightly browning the fish on both sides, for about 3 minutes per side, then add the white wine. When the wine has evaporated to a few table-spoons, add the tomato, basil, capers, and olives. Cook for 1 to 2 minutes to allow the tomato to release its liquid, then for another minute to reduce slightly. Remove the pan from the heat.

Serve the fish with the rice, topped with the tomato, caper, and olive pan sauce.

MAURIZIO SUGGESTS: A dry, not too fruity white, such as Pinot Grigio from Friuli, is a refreshing partner for such assertive flavors.

Over the years, authors and Italian food and wine experts Marcella and Victor Hazan have become dear friends. Marcella and Mara are kindred spirits in the kitchen—if they're not cooking together, they're talking about food at a level of excitement reserved for schoolgirls! One day, Marcella was raving about a dish she had tried in Rome, a city famous for its artichokes and mazzancolle shrimp, which had been roasted under a bed of melted mozzarella. Mara's mouth was watering just thinking about it, so when the artichokes from Sant' Erasmo were in season some months later, and the scampi were at their sweetest, she created a Venetian version. For cheese, she turned to fresh scamorza, a denser cow's milk cheese that melts into a creamy blanket and has a slightly stronger, grassier flavor.

This is one of our favorite dishes to serve guests at home, since everything can be prepared before we sit down to eat. Since it combines fish, cheese, and vegetables, it's an ideal *piatto unico*—all-in-one course. Serve with a green salad.

Shrimp, Artichoke, and Scamorza Cheese "Pot Pie"

Gratinata di Scampi con Carciofi e Scamorza *Makes 4 servings*

10 baby artichokes
¼ cup extra virgin olive oil
1 garlic clove, crushed
Salt and freshly ground black pepper
½ cup dry white wine
2 tablespoons chopped flat-leaf parsley
32 medium shrimp, peeled and deveined
6 ounces Scamorza cheese, thinly sliced
½ cup grated Parmigiano-Reggiano
½ cup finely ground unseasoned breadcrumbs (see page 32)

Cut the stems and the spiny tops of the leaves from the artichokes. Starting at the base, bend the leaves back and snap them off where they break naturally; continue until all the tough outer leaves have been removed, leaving a cone of tender pale green leaves. Using a small sharp knife, trim the outside edge of the base until smooth and no dark green areas remain. Cut the artichoke in half lengthwise. Using a small knife, cut out any choke (there will be very little in baby artichokes) and small purple-tipped leaves from each half. Cut the cleaned artichoke halves into thin slices.

Preheat the oven to 425°F.

Heat the oil in a large skillet over medium-high heat. Add the artichoke slices and garlic and season with salt and pepper; cook, tossing or stirring, for 3 to 4 minutes. Discard the garlic. Add the white wine and let it evaporate to a tablespoon or two, then add the parsley with enough water to cover the artichokes. Simmer until the artichokes are tender and the liquid has evaporated, about 10 minutes.

Spread the artichokes in one layer on the bottom and halfway up the sides of four 5- to 6-inch round or oval baking or gratin dishes. Place 3 shrimp on each side with their tails meeting in the center, then arrange 3 shrimp down the line where their tails touch. Season the shrimp with salt and pepper, then layer the Scamorza cheese over the top. Dust with the Parmigiano and breadcrumbs. Place the baking dishes in the oven and cook until the tops just start to brown and bubble, 8 to 10 minutes. Place the baking dishes on charger plates and serve.

Artichokes

*U*NLIKE THE ROUNDER, bright green globe artichokes from California, our celebrated *castraure* (or *carciofini* in Italian) are longer and thinner, with soft purple and light green hues brushed along the tops of the leaves. They're also a fraction of the size, just a few inches long at most, and have a delicate texture and pronounced bitter flavor that dissipates after cooking. Best of all, they're virtually choke-free, so the entire vegetable can be eaten. Small or baby artichokes are becoming more available in the United States.

As their Venetian name suggests, these tiny specimens are the result of a vegetal "castration" of sorts. Farmers remove the early top flower, or *castraure,* when the artichoke plant contains just a few buds in the early spring—there's only one per plant, which explains why they're so prized. The plant goes through two other phases after the top flower has been snipped, the *botoli,* or small artichokes in the middle of the plant will grow to a medium size, and the ones on the bottom, the carciofi (in our dialect, *articioco*) will become larger artichokes.

For centuries, *castraure* were unique to the Venetian lagoon. Though farmers near the Ligurian coast have started growing them (because of the warmer climate, they come to market sooner than ours), the ones from Sant' Erasmo and Torcello in our lagoon are prized for their intense, slightly briny flavor.

When Mara started working with fish fillets, these tender red mullet rolls were one of her first fortuitous experiments. As elemental as this dish is, embellished with nothing more than a tangle of spinach, a few bittersweet radicchio leaves, and the essence of the fish released in the pan, the effect is as sensational today as it was twenty years ago.

Rolled Red Mullet with Radicchio and Spinach

Rotoli di Triglia con Radicchio di Treviso e Spinaci   *Makes 4 servings*

3 tablespoons unsalted butter
Twelve 1½- to 2-ounce fillets red mullet (if small fillets are
    not available, substitute six 3- to 4-ounce fillets and halve
    them)
Salt and freshly ground black pepper
1 garlic clove, crushed
2 pounds baby spinach, cleaned
2 tablespoons chopped chives
2 tablespoons chopped flat-leaf parsley
¼ cup finely ground fresh breadcrumbs (see page 32)
2 tablespoons extra virgin olive oil plus more for drizzling
1 to 1½ cups Fish Broth (page 14)
4 leaves radicchio di Treviso, julienned

Preheat the oven to 450°F. Grease a glass or ceramic baking dish with a tablespoon of the butter. Season the red mullet fillets with salt and pepper, then roll them lengthwise and secure with a toothpick.

Heat the remaining 2 tablespoons of the butter and the garlic in a large skillet over medium heat. When the garlic just starts to brown, discard and add the spinach leaves, season with salt, and cook, tossing or gently stirring, until the released water has evaporated, 3 to 4 minutes. Set aside, leaving the spinach in the pan to keep it warm.

Place the fish in the baking dish. Sprinkle the chives, parsley, and breadcrumbs over the top. Lightly drizzle with olive oil. Add enough broth to the bottom of the pan to reach ½ inch up the sides of the fish. Place the pan in the oven and cook until the fish is just opaque, 10 to 12 minutes.

Place a mound of spinach in the center of each serving plate, then flatten it slightly. Arrange three red mullet rolls over the spinach. Season the radicchio with salt and drizzle with the 2 tablespoons oil. Garnish the plate with a small mound of the julienned radicchio and serve.

Red Mullet

MARA *at the* **FISH MARKET**

*W*ITH PINK-HUED SKIN and rich flesh, Adriatic red mullet *(triglie)* is one of our favorite fish. We use two kinds in Venice: *triglie di fango,* or "of the mud," are also known as *barbone,* with two whiskers that hang down like a beard. These are the specimens found in our shallow waters, around the Gulf of Venezia. *Triglie di scoglio,* or "of the rocks," with its brinier, more flavorful and compact meat, is slightly larger and is common along the Adriatic's eastern shore. Both kinds are easy to fillet, although they're most often cooked whole and served one or two per person.

Although not always easy to find, Mediterranean and Adriatic red mullet is now available in North American fish markets. Weighing in at about 5 ounces whole, the tiny fillets are about 1½ ounces each. Your fishmonger will fillet them for you, but they're simple to clean at this size. The Mediterranean variety, called rouget, is prized for its unique flavor, which is sweeter and more delicate the smaller the fish. Larger domestic fillets (3 to 4 ounces) are more common; you can halve or cut them into thirds to replicate our smaller fillets.

Ripe figs become sweeter when baked alongside these delicate red mullet fillets. Many Venetian recipes that now call for tomatoes, a New World ingredient, originally called for the sweet, slightly acidic flavor of figs. You can use any kind of fig—Black Mission figs, or sweet green or white ones, but the riper they are, the softer they'll become, and the richer the pan juices will be. A sprinkle of fresh mint gives this summer dish a refreshing lift.

Red Mullet Stars with Fresh Figs and Mint

Stelle di Triglie con Fichi e Menta *Makes 4 servings*

8 fresh figs
4 tablespoons extra virgin olive oil
Twenty 1½- to 2-ounce red mullet fillets (if small fillets are not
    available, purchase ten 3- to 4-ounce fillets and halve them)
2 tablespoons snipped chives
2 tablespoons chopped flat-leaf parsley
1 large ripe tomato (about 6 ounces), peeled, seeded, and diced
Salt and freshly ground black pepper
⅓ cup finely ground fresh breadcrumbs (see page 32)
8 leaves mint, cut into thin ribbons

Preheat the oven to 450°F. Remove the stems from the figs. Using a sharp paring knife, peel the skin, then cut an X incision in the top of each fig. The depth of the cut should extend to the point where the fig expands out into a bulb, about an inch. Set aside.

Spread 2 tablespoons of the oil on the bottom of a large baking dish or shallow roasting pan. Place the red mullet fillets in one layer on the bottom. Add the figs around the sides. Sprinkle the fish and the figs with the chives, parsley, and tomato and season with salt and pepper. Sprinkle the top with breadcrumbs and drizzle with the remaining 2 tablespoons oil. Place the pan in the oven and bake uncovered until lightly browned and the fish is just cooked, 8 to 10 minutes.

Place 2 figs in the center of each serving plate. Using a spatula, arrange 5 red mullet fillets around the figs, forming a "star." Spoon the pan sauce over the fish, sprinkle with the mint, and serve immediately.

Mara designed this lighter version of fried scampi—a traditional delight served at many of Venice's cicheti bars—for Maurizio, who can never seem to get enough of them. Dredged in flour, dipped in citrus-fragranced beaten egg, coated with fresh herb breadcrumbs and roasted, these crispy crusts conceal sweet scampi but their delicate taste isn't overwhelmed by oil or butter. We serve these with tiny cherry tomatoes sliced in half, sprinkled with breadcrumbs, and roasted alongside the scampi.

Scampi, which also go by the names Dublin Bay prawn langoustines and Norwegian shrimp, are available fresh and frozen from North American fishmongers. Jumbo shrimp can be substituted.

Jumbo Shrimp in Bread "Shirt" with Aromatic Herbs

Scampi in Camicia di Pane e Erbe Aromatiche   *Makes 4 servings*

20 jumbo shrimp with heads on
3 large eggs
Grated zest of 1 orange
2 cups finely ground fresh breadcrumbs (see page 32)
2 tablespoons chopped chives
2 tablespoons chopped rosemary leaves
2 tablespoons chopped thyme leaves
1 tablespoon chopped sage
2 cups all-purpose flour
Salt
12 cherry tomatoes, halved lengthwise
Extra virgin olive oil for drizzling

Preheat the oven to 450°F. Grease a casserole or baking pan with olive oil. Set aside.

Rinse the shrimp under cold running water. Pull off the shell from the body and the tail, but leave the head on.

In a small bowl, beat the eggs with the grated orange zest. Set aside.

In another small shallow bowl mix the breadcrumbs with the herbs. Set aside. Put the flour in a third shallow bowl.

Season the shrimp with salt. One at a time, dredge them in the flour, shaking off any excess, followed by the egg mixture, then the breadcrumbs. Reserve the leftover breadcrumbs. As the shrimp are coated, place them in the casserole or baking dish. Add the tomato halves, cut side up. Sprinkle some of the remaining breadcrumbs over the tomatoes. Drizzle the shrimp and tomatoes with olive oil.

Place the baking dish in the oven and cook uncovered until the shrimp and tops of the tomatoes are lightly browned, 7 to 8 minutes. Arrange 5 shrimp and 6 tomato halves on each serving plate.

MAURIZIO SUGGESTS: A dry, full-bodied white wine with crisp citrus notes, such as a Ribolla Gialla Orientale del Friuli.

Tuna is the steak of the fish world. Rich, red, and meaty, its best qualities shine when quickly seared and left rare in the center, then thinly sliced and fanned out on a plate. A drizzle of rosemary oil lends a deep, piney warmth. The accompanying beans, neatly bundled with smoked pancetta, are just a suggestion—you can serve this tuna with any seasonal vegetable. The rosemary oil, made with mild extra virgin olive oil, will keep for up to two months stored in a cool, dark place. It's also wonderful drizzled over grilled steaks, roasted vegetables, and toasted bread. Purchase the firm, moist, sushi-grade tuna for this recipe: we prefer *pinna gialla,* or yellowfin tuna that's caught just outside Venice.

Seared Tuna Slices with Rosemary

Tagliata di Tonno al Rosmarino   *Makes 4 servings*

2 cups extra virgin olive oil plus 1 tablespoon for cooking
   the tuna
½ cup chopped rosemary leaves
2 teaspoons crushed hot red pepper
1 garlic clove
Salt
¾ pound French beans or haricots verts, ends trimmed
8 thin slices smoked pancetta
1½ pounds tuna loin, cut into a square block by your
   fishmonger
Salt and freshly ground black pepper

Optional Garnish
¼ recipe da Fiore Batter (page 59)
4 large sprigs rosemary
Corn or sunflower oil for frying

At least 2 days (and up to 2 weeks) in advance, prepare the rosemary-seasoned oil by combining the 2 cups olive oil, the rosemary, crushed red pepper, and garlic. Season with salt. Strain the oil through cheesecloth into a clean jar and seal until ready to use.

Bring a large pot of water to a boil. Season with salt and add the beans. Cook until tender but still firm, about 5 minutes, then drain. Transfer the beans to a bowl of ice water to cool. Drain well. Wrap 5 to 6 beans with a piece of the pancetta, making a neat package. Set aside.

Cut the tuna loin into four "logs." This will give you a more even surface to sear and a better presentation. Heat the tablespoon of oil in a large skillet over medium-high heat. When almost smoking, add the tuna logs and the pancetta-wrapped beans. Partially cover the pan and cook, searing the tuna on all sides, about a minute per side, and turning the beans as you turn the tuna; the tuna should be medium-rare. Remove the tuna logs from the pan and set aside briefly.

If preparing the garnish in a Dutch oven or deep-fat fryer, heat the oil over medium heat until a deep-fat thermometer registers 350°F (very hot but not smoking). Dip the rosemary in water, then in flour, shake, dip in the batter, and transfer to the hot oil. Cook until lightly brown and crisp, 1 to 2 minutes.

Transfer two packages of beans to each serving plate. Using a sharp knife, cut the tuna in very thin slices, ¼ inch thick or less. Fan out 10 to 12 slices around three-fourths of the edge of the plate, across from the beans. Season the tuna with salt and pepper and drizzle with the infused rosemary oil. Place the fried rosemary in the center of each serving plate.

MAURIZIO SUGGESTS: Since this dish is similar to a good steak, I pour a dry, aged red wine. Steer away from those with heavy tannins that will overpower the fish—a Valpolicella is my first pick.

Our holiday menus are our most elaborate and indulgent. Winter appetites welcome bold, layered flavors—in this case, leeks, cured ham, and grouper. Guests who don't usually like broccoli love this sumptuous soufflé, which is the focal point of the dish. Mara's soufflé recipe is foolproof—in fact, it's really more of a *tortino*, or dense custard. Italian guanciale, like many cured, ready-to-eat pork products, is not permitted into the United States. Instead, use a meaty pancetta.

Guanciale-Wrapped Grouper with Broccoli and Thyme Soufflé

Cernia alla Mara Martin   *Makes 4 servings*

3 leeks

5 ounces broccoli florets (about 1½ cups)

1 small potato (about 4 ounces), peeled and cut into
    quarters

3 tablespoons extra virgin olive oil

½ small onion, thinly sliced

2 teaspoons chopped thyme

Salt and freshly ground black pepper

2 tablespoons unsalted butter

2 tablespoons all-purpose flour

1 cup hot milk

⅓ cup grated Parmigiano-Reggiano

Pinch ground nutmeg

8 large eggs

Four 6-ounce grouper fillets

16 long, thin slices guanciale (substitute pancetta if
    unavailable)

1 cup Fish Broth (page 14) or water

Bring a large pot of water to a boil, then season with salt. Trim the root ends and dark green parts from the leeks. Slice the remaining white and light green parts in half lengthwise into "leaves" and thoroughly clean. Separate the leaves, selecting sixteen long whole pieces. Blanch the leaves in the boiling water until tender, 3 to 4 minutes. Using tongs or a skimmer, transfer the leaves to a bowl of ice water to quickly cool. Drain and set aside. Keep the water in the pot at a low boil. Add the broccoli and potato and cook until tender but still firm, about 5 minutes. Reserve a cup of the cooking liquid. Drain and set aside.

Preheat the oven to 400°F. Butter four 4-ounce ramekins or soufflé molds.

In a medium skillet, heat the olive oil over medium-high heat. Add the onion and cook, stirring often, until softened, 3 to 4 minutes. Add the broccoli, potato, and a teaspoon of the thyme, and season with salt and pepper; cook, tossing or stirring, for a minute, then add the reserved cooking liquid. Simmer, partially covered, until the broccoli and potato are very soft, about 15 minutes; a sharp paring knife should be easily inserted and the liquid almost completely evaporated. Set aside to cool slightly.

Meanwhile, in a medium heavy saucepan prepare the béchamel. Melt the butter over low heat. When it starts to foam, add the flour all at once, mixing well with a wooden spoon. Add the hot milk and simmer, stirring gently with a wire whisk or wooden spoon. Cook, stirring, over low heat, 5 to 8 minutes, until smooth and thickened. Remove from the heat, stir in the Parmigiano, and season with salt and nutmeg to taste. Cool slightly.

Work the potato and broccoli through a sieve into a large bowl, or, in a food processor, combine ⅓ cup of the béchamel and the broccoli and potato mixture. Puree until smooth. Add the béchamel (or the remaining béchamel if a food processor is used) to the broccoli and potato paste. One by one, add the eggs, whisking to incorporate with each addition. Using a ladle, fill the prepared ramekins two-thirds full with the broccoli mixture. Place the ramekins in a shallow baking dish and add enough hot water to come halfway up the sides. Bake until the soufflés are puffed and set, 18 to 20 minutes.

While the soufflés cook, prepare the fish by cutting each fillet into four approximately 1½-ounce pieces. Season the chunks of grouper with salt and pepper and sprinkle with the remaining teaspoon of thyme. Lay the blanched leek leaves flat on a work surface. Place a piece of seasoned fish at one end and roll closed; repeat until you have sixteen leek-wrapped "packages." Roll each package in a piece of guanciale or pancetta and place in a baking pan just large enough to hold the packages in one layer without touching. Pour about ¼-inch of fish broth or water in the bottom of the pan and bake uncovered 12 to 15 minutes, until the fish is cooked.

Serve the soufflé, lightly drizzled with olive oil, on one side of a serving dish with four pieces of grouper surrounding it.

In this signature dish, the fish retains its moisture while steaming, thanks to the lettuce-leaf wrapping. Select a sturdy lettuce, such as green leaf or Boston lettuce that retains its color and texture. You can use a Chinese steamer if you prefer, but a simple insert works just as well. An Aceto Balsamico Tradizionale di Modena aged at least thirty years with a thick, syrupy consistency works best.

Steamed Sea Bass with Stewed Apples and Aged Balsamic Vinegar

Branzino al Vapore con Mele e Aceto Balsamico Tradizionale di Modena

Makes 4 servings

2 cups dry white wine

2 cups water

1 tablespoon salt

8 large whole lettuce leaves

Four 6-ounce fillets sea bass

Salt and freshly ground black pepper

2 apples, peeled, cored, and cut into ½-inch-thick wedges

Aged balsamic vinegar from Modena for drizzling

Extra virgin olive oil

8 fresh bay leaves

In a medium saucepan combine the wine, water, and salt. Bring to a boil. Add the lettuce leaves, taking care not to break them. Almost immediately, after about 5 seconds, carefully remove the lettuce and transfer to an ice bath. Reserve the cooking liquid. Remove the lettuce from the ice water and spread the leaves out on a clean work surface. Pat dry.

Season the bass fillets with salt and pepper. Place one bass fillet on a lettuce leaf. Place another leaf on top and tuck the edges under the fillet. Bring the bottom edges up, forming a neat bundle. Repeat with the remaining fillets.

Place a steamer insert over the reserved cooking liquid or transfer the liquid to a steamer. Bring to a moderate boil and place the wrapped fillets on the insert. Cover and cook until the fish is just cooked through, 10 to 12 minutes. During the last 5 minutes of cooking, add the apple wedges to the steamer.

To serve, place a 4- to 5-inch circle of slightly overlapping apple wedges in the center of each plate. Set the fish on top. Drizzle with balsamic vinegar and olive oil, garnish with the bay leaves, and serve immediately.

MAURIZIO SUGGESTS: The balsamic vinegar, even if aged and almost sweet, tends to upstage the taste of most wines, so we recommend a light, simple red or white like Valpolicella or Soave.

Sea Bass

THE SILVER SEA BASS from the Adriatic is one of the stars of the Venetian table. Its soft, lean flesh has a distinct yet delicate flavor. In Venice, the prized smaller ones are often grilled for individual servings, while larger *branzini* make a festive meal for three or four when roasted in the oven. Called *spigola* in Italian, bass are saltwater fish that reproduce in fresh water, and between July and December our lagoon is full of them. The farm-raised specimens are available all year, although their flavor is not as intense as wild sea bass. Striped bass is the best substitute in North America, if you can't find fresh Adriatic branzino (or branzini, bronzino, bronzini—there are many spelling permutations)!

Our North American guests share our gusto for soft-shell crabs but are always surprised—and thrilled—to find out what tiny delicacies ours are, compared to those available along their East Coast. Just one or two inches long, these tiny crabs are the pride of the lagoon in the fall and spring when they shed their shells. The crab fishermen who hail from Burano and Torcello catch these crabs and put them in underwater boxes. Every day, they check to see if the crabs have shed their shells yet, and usher them to the market at the exact moment they molt. The females shed their shells only in the autumn and are best in October and November when they contain their roe.

Traditionally, handfuls of live crabs are placed in a batter of egg and Parmigiano for an hour so that when they're fried, they puff up inside and out. Prepared this way, the batter, not the delicate crabmeat, is what you taste. Instead, Mara uses a lighter batter and accompanies the crabs with a zippy orange-arugula salad tossed with peppery Tuscan oil.

Though significantly larger, soft-shell blue crabs are extraordinary when prepared this way. They're available at seafood markets in many sizes. All work well. There's a smaller size that's closest to our *moleche* called Buster that rarely makes it to the retail counter, although many seafood purveyors can order them for you.

Fried Soft-Shell Crabs on Arugula and Orange Salad

Frittura di Moleche con Insalata d'Arance Rucola   *Makes 4 servings*

12 small soft-shell crabs
2 oranges
2 lemons
1 recipe da Fiore Batter (page 59), chilled with 3 to 4 ice cubes
2 quarts corn or sunflower oil for frying
Salt
6 cups baby arugula, cleaned
4 tablespoons extra virgin olive oil
Salt and freshly ground black pepper

To clean the crabs, peel back the pointed part of the shell and scrape away the gills from each side. Holding the crab in the palm of your hand, use kitchen shears or sharp scissors to cut off the head.

Squeeze out the green bubble behind the eyes. Bend back the "apron," the thin flap on the underside of the crab. Twist the apron until it breaks off. Rinse the crab with water and drain.

Carefully peel the oranges and lemons, removing all the bitter white pith and completely exposing the bright flesh. Using a sharp paring knife, remove the segments from the membranes by sliding the knife on both sides, then lifting the segment out. Place in a bowl; set aside.

In a large Dutch oven or deep-fat fryer, heat the oil over medium heat until a deep-fat thermometer registers 350°F (very hot but not smoking).

One by one, pass the crabs through the flour; shake off any excess, then immerse in the cold batter. One by one, carefully place the batter-coated crabs in the hot oil. Cook, in two to three batches, until crisp and golden brown, about 2 minutes per side. As they cook, transfer the crabs to a paper towel–lined sheet pan and lightly season with salt.

To serve, place a mound of arugula on each serving plate and scatter some orange and lemon segments over the top. Drizzle with olive oil and season with salt and pepper. Top each salad with three soft-shell crabs and serve.

MAURIZIO SUGGESTS: A young, dry white wine that's light and fruity, such as Tocai Friulano or a great Soave.

Fennel's crunchy stalks and feathery fronds lend a compellingly sweet, anise-like flavor to Mara's imperial shrimp stuffing, which she conceals in *seppioline*, tiny cuttlefish. When they first swim into the lagoon, the thimble-size cuttlefish are too small to stuff. We wait until August, when they grow to about three inches and still have an incredibly sweet and delicate flavor. As they cook, the inner cuttlebone juts up as the skin around it contracts, making them look like tiny sailboats. Calamari don't have the same whimsical effect, but their size, shape, and taste works just as well.

Since imperial shrimp are hard to find, use smaller, sweet shrimp: if they're too large, their texture becomes too chewy for the stuffing. If you find small cuttlefish about three inches long, the size of calamari, clean them as described on page 174, with a few adjustments. Leave the shell intact, and remove just the skin that surrounds it. Using your finger, reach into the body opening and pull out the ink sac. You don't need it for this recipe. You can leave the marrone, the maroon sac, as it lends a rich flavor.

Squid Stuffed with Fennel and Imperial Shrimp

Seppie Ripiene di Finocchi e Mazzancolle   *Makes 4 servings*

2 small zucchini

½ recipe baked rice (page 17)

4 tablespoons extra virgin olive oil plus more for drizzling

1½ cups diced fennel (about 2 bulbs)

2 garlic cloves, crushed

Salt and freshly ground black pepper

6 ounces *mazzancolle* or imperial shrimp, peeled and
    deveined

1 large egg, beaten

¾ cup unseasoned breadcrumbs (see page 32)

12 baby calamari or cuttlefish, cleaned (if unavailable,
    cut 6 large calamari in half)

½ cup grated Parmigiano-Reggiano

¾ to 1 cup Fish Broth (page 14) or water

Cut each zucchini crosswise into two sections, discarding the ends, and with a melon baller scoop out the center of each section, leaving ¼-inch-thick shells and bottom and reserving the centers for another use. In a steamer set over simmering water, steam the zucchini shells, covered, for 4 minutes, or until barely tender but still bright green. Transfer the shells to paper towels to drain upside down. When cool enough to handle, stuff the zucchini shells with the baked rice. Set aside.

To prepare the stuffing for the calamari, heat 2 tablespoons of the olive oil in a medium skillet over medium-high heat. Add the fennel and a garlic clove and season with salt and pepper. Cook, stirring often, until the fennel softens; add a tablespoon or two of water, if necessary, to continue cooking until soft, about 8 minutes. Discard the garlic. Transfer the mixture to a medium bowl; set aside to cool.

Cut the shrimp into small pieces. Heat the remaining 2 tablespoons olive oil and the remaining garlic clove in a medium-skillet over medium-high heat. When the garlic just turns golden, add the shrimp, season with salt and pepper, and cook, tossing or stirring, until the shrimp is just cooked, about 2 minutes. Discard the garlic and transfer the shrimp to the bowl with the fennel.

Mix the egg into the fennel and shrimp mixture. Stir in ¼ cup of the breadcrumbs. The mixture should be a thick paste; add a few more breadcrumbs and adjust the seasoning with salt and pepper, if necessary. Stuff the calamari with the filling.

Preheat the oven to 425°F.

Rub the bottom of a baking pan with oil and place the stuffed calamari on the bottom. Sprinkle half the remaining breadcrumbs and half the Parmigiano over the calamari. Drizzle the tops with olive oil. Add just enough fish broth or water to the baking dish to create a thin (⅛ inch or less) layer on the bottom of the pan. Bake uncovered for 10 minutes, then add the stuffed zucchini; sprinkle with the remaining breadcrumbs and Parmigiano and drizzle with olive oil. Cook for another 5 minutes till the calamari become golden.

This is one of Mara's most popular recipes at da Fiore, and one she often prepares for dinner parties at home, since everything can be done ahead of time. One sole fillet is topped with baked rice and porcini mushrooms, then covered with another fillet and baked on a bed of artichokes. Venetians prefer sole when they are just a few inches long in late summer and early fall, but larger specimens available in North America are a fine substitute.

Sole with Porcini and Artichoke

Tasca di Sogliola con Porcini e Carciofi   *Makes 4 servings*

4 ounces fresh porcini mushrooms, cleaned and sliced, or
    ½ ounce dried
1 lemon, halved
4 medium artichokes
3 tablespoons unsalted butter plus some for coating the
    baking dish
½ cup dry white wine
½ cup water
2 tablespoons chopped flat-leaf parsley
Grated zest of 1 lemon
Salt and freshly ground black pepper
8 fillets of sole or substitute flounder
½ recipe baked rice (page 17)
⅓ cup unseasoned breadcrumbs (see page 32)
1 cup Fish Broth (page 14) or water
1 sprig thyme

If using dried porcini mushrooms, place them in a bowl, cover with water, and soak for at least 30 minutes. Lift the mushrooms from the soaking liquid, chop them into small pieces, and add them to the baked rice recipe when you add the rice.

Squeeze the juice from the lemon halves into a large bowl; add the lemon halves. Fill the bowl with water. Cut the stem and sharp tips off an artichoke. Starting at the base, bend the leaves back and snap them off where they break naturally; continue until all the tough outer leaves have been removed, leaving a cone of tender, pale yellow-green leaves. Cut the top leaves off, leaving just the artichoke bottom.

Trim the dark green fibrous parts from the base and sides of the artichoke with a sharp paring knife, rounding it into a smooth puck. Using a small knife, cut out the choke and small purple-tipped leaves from the center. Rub the cut areas with lemon. Place in the lemon water. Repeat with the remaining artichokes.

Preheat the oven to 400°F. Butter the bottom of an 11 × 7 × 1½-inch baking dish. Set aside.

In a small baking dish or casserole, combine the white wine, water, parsley, and lemon zest. Remove the artichoke bottoms from the water and add them to the dish. Season with salt and pepper and cover the dish tightly with foil. Place the dish in the oven and cook until a paring knife easily pierces the base of an artichoke, about 25 minutes.

Meanwhile, stuff the fillets of sole. Place four of the fillets on a clean, flat work surface. Season with salt and pepper, then spoon a ½-inch-thick layer of the baked rice on top; leave a ½-inch margin around the sides. Top the rice-lined fillet with another fillet and gently press the sides down to seal. Repeat with the remaining fillets and rice. Place the stuffed fillets in the prepared baking dish. Lightly dust the fish with breadcrumbs, then dot the tops with the 3 tablespoons butter. Add just enough fish broth to reach ¼ inch up the sides of the fish. Add the thyme sprig to the pan and bake until the fish is lightly brown and the edges easily flake, about 15 minutes. Serve immediately with the artichoke bottoms.

MAURIZIO SUGGESTS: Artichokes are difficult to pair with wine, but a dry, young white with a crisp, balanced acidity, such as Tocai Friulano, is a good choice.

Is it more than just a culinary coincidence that Venetian calamari are perfectly sized for stuffing and at their peak of flavor during chestnut season? The Veneto is blanketed with centuries-old chestnut groves, and country cooks like Mara's grandmother are fond of fragrant stuffings for poultry made with their sweet, meaty flavor. With its tubular shape, calamari is the perfect Venetian alternative.

A pastry bag makes easy work of the stuffing. Snip off the very tip of the other end of the calamari so that the steam can escape—otherwise, they may rupture while cooking. Prepare the chestnuts up to a day in advance. Stuff the calamari fifteen minutes before you're ready to eat, drizzle with Ligurian oil, and place the pan in the oven. We serve three to a plate with a scoop of baked rice and the rich pan juices.

Chestnut-Filled Calamari

Calamari Ripieni di Castagne   *Makes 4 servings*

¾ pound fresh chestnuts
12 whole medium calamari, cut in half if large
3 tablespoons extra virgin olive oil plus more for drizzling
1 garlic clove, crushed
⅓ cup dry white wine
1 tablespoon thyme leaves
Salt
2 to 3 cups Fish Broth (page 14)
⅓ cup unseasoned breadcrumbs (see page 32)
Unsalted butter for coating the baking dish
1 tablespoon chopped flat-leaf parsley

Prepare the chestnuts by using a sharp paring knife to make a lengthwise incision on their curved side. Put them in a bowl and cover with cold water. Set aside for 2 hours.

Clean the calamari by holding the body in one hand while gently pulling on the tentacles to remove the insides. Remove the quill from inside the body cavity and peel the skin away from the outside of the body. Once the insides are out, pull or cut the head away from the tentacles. Wash the tentacles and body under cold running water. Cut the tentacles into small pieces; leave the body whole. Reserve separately. Set aside.

Preheat the oven to 350°F.

Drain the chestnuts and place in a roasting pan (use two pans, if necessary, to hold them in one layer). Roast until they split open and are well browned, about 50 minutes. When they are cool enough to handle, peel away and discard the shell and outer skin. Chop the chestnuts into small pieces. This may be done up to a day in advance. If using immediately, increase the oven temperature to 425°F.

Heat the olive oil and garlic in a large skillet over medium-high heat. When the garlic just starts to brown, about a minute, remove and discard. Add the chopped calamari tentacles and cook, stirring, until they lightly brown, 1 to 2 minutes. Add the white wine, allowing it to evaporate to a tablespoon or two. Add the chestnuts and a teaspoon of the thyme and season with salt. Cook, tossing or stirring, for a minute, then add 1⅓ cups of the broth. Bring to a boil, then reduce the heat and simmer for 30 minutes. Stir in ¼ cup of the breadcrumbs. The mixture should be dense and pasty. Set aside to cool before stuffing the calamari.

Transfer the filling to a pastry bag fitted with a wide round tip. Fill each tubular calamari with the stuffing. Using kitchen scissors or a sharp knife, trim off the pointed end of each calamari. This will release the steam from the filling as it cooks. Butter the bottom of a baking dish just large enough to hold the filled calamari in one layer. Add the calamari. Sprinkle with the parsley and the remaining breadcrumbs and thyme. Lightly drizzle oil over each calamari. Add just enough broth to come ½ inch up the sides of the calamari. Place the pan in the oven and roast for 12 to 15 minutes, until lightly browned and heated through. Place three calamari on each serving plate and drizzle with the juices in the baking pan. Serve with baked rice (page 17).

MAURIZIO SUGGESTS: A dry, mature, full-bodied white, preferably aged in wood with a nice bitterish aftertaste—Pinot Bianco, for example.

This is one of our oldest and simplest summer recipes: tender matchsticks of zucchini wrapped in sweet sole fillets with basil leaf ribbons. With a bit of fish broth and a drizzle of light Ligurian oil, each ingredient shines. If you're working with whole sole, fillet the fish (or ask your fishmonger to do it) and prepare a broth using the head and bones.

Rolled Fillet of Sole with Zucchini

Involtini di Sogliola con Zucchini 🌸 *Makes 4 servings*

2 small zucchini, halved and cut into approximately
   3-inch-long by ¼-inch-thick sticks
Four 5- to 6-ounce sole fillets
Salt and freshly ground black pepper
8 basil leaves, cut into thin ribbons
Extra virgin olive oil to coat baking dish plus more
   for drizzling
¼ cup unseasoned breadcrumbs (see page 32)
2 tablespoons chopped chives
Approximately 1 cup Fish Broth (page 14)

Preheat the oven to 450°F.

Cook the zucchini in boiling salted water for 3 minutes. Drain. Quickly cool by transferring to a bowl of ice water. Drain and set aside.

Season the sole fillets with salt and pepper and sprinkle with the basil. Place five to six of the blanched zucchini sticks more than 2 inches from one end of the fish fillet, then fold the end over the zucchini and roll closed.

Coat a baking dish with oil and place the zucchini-filled sole in the pan, seam side down. Sprinkle with the breadcrumbs and chives. Season with salt and pepper and drizzle olive oil over the top. Add just enough fish broth to cover the bottom of the baking dish by ¼ inch. Bake until the fish is lightly browned and easily flakes, 10 to 12 minutes.

With a blanket of golden crisp, paper-thin potato slices fanned out over the fillet, our roasted turbot is a da Fiore favorite. The potatoes hold the delicate flatfish fillets together, seal in the turbot's moisture, and soak up the flavorful juices that do manage to escape. Turbot, which is similar to our *rombo,* is readily available whole, so you should make a very flavorful broth out of the bones and head. Substitute halibut if turbot is unavailable. Practically every ounce of this delicious show-stopper can be prepared ahead of time, making this a wonderful dinner party dish.

Roasted Turbot in Potato Crust

Rombo al Forno in Crosta di Patate   *Makes 4 servings*

Turbot Broth
1 pound head and bones from turbot, well rinsed
1 celery stalk, halved
1 carrot, quartered
½ small onion
2 quarts water
Salt

Turbot
2 tablespoons extra virgin olive oil plus more for drizzling
2 large baking potatoes
One 750-ml bottle dry white wine
1 quart water
Salt
Four 5- to 6-ounce turbot fillets
2 tablespoons finely chopped chives plus ¼ cup
2 tablespoons finely chopped flat-leaf parsley plus ¼ cup
1 large egg beaten with 2 tablespoons water
⅓ cup unseasoned breadcrumbs (see page 32)

5 tablespoons unsalted butter
¼ cup plus 1 tablespoon all-purpose flour
½ cup finely chopped basil
2 cups hot turbot broth (see above)

To prepare the broth, place the fish head and bones, celery, carrot, and onion in a large pot. Cover with the water and season with salt. Bring to a boil, then reduce the heat and simmer for 30 minutes, skimming the surface frequently to remove the foamy scum or impurities. Using a ladle, strain the stock through a fine-mesh strainer into a container. If not using immediately, cool in an ice bath, then cover and refrigerate for up to 2 days.

Preheat the oven to 450°F. Lightly coat with the oil a shallow baking pan large enough to hold the turbot fillets in one layer without touching.

Wash and peel the potatoes, then cut into paper-thin slices on a mandoline or the wide slicer of a box grater. In a medium saucepan, combine the wine and the water and season with salt. Bring to a boil. Add the potatoes and cook for 30 seconds. Drain into a colander immediately. Transfer the potato slices to a bowl of ice water. Drain again.

Season the fillets with salt and sprinkle with the 2 tablespoons chives and 2 tablespoons parsley. Wrap each fillet completely in sliced potatoes, overlapping the slices across the width of the fillet. Lightly brush with the egg wash and sprinkle the tops with the breadcrumbs. Drizzle the potato-wrapped fillets with olive oil. Pour the turbot broth into the pan to a depth of ¼ inch. Place the pan in the oven and roast for 15 minutes or until the potatoes are crisp and golden. As the fish cooks, prepare the sauce.

To prepare a roux, melt the butter in a medium saucepan over medium heat. Add the flour, stirring to incorporate. Stir in the basil and ¼ cup each of chives and parsley; cook, stirring with a wooden spoon, until the flour becomes lightly golden, 4 to 5 minutes. Do not allow the roux to brown. Slowly add the fish broth, whisking to incorporate. Bring the sauce to a boil, then lower the heat to a simmer and cook, stirring, until the sauce is thick enough to coat the back of a spoon, about 5 minutes. Season to taste with salt.

Serve the potato-crusted turbot with the herb sauce.

Salt-encrusted fish recipes date to the Venetian Republic's monopoly on salt. This method always yields moist, delectable results. While the hardened salt seals in the fish juices, keeping the flesh tender, the layer of lemons imparts a subtle citrus flavor and prevents the fillets from absorbing too much of the salt. The piney aroma of rosemary permeates the fish.

Use any round, white-fleshed fish with this salt crust, but *branzino* (sea bass) is our favorite. We serve this with vegetables, boiled or steamed potatoes, and a homemade mayonnaise containing chopped chives and rosemary.

Roasted Sea Bass in Salt Crust

Branzino al Sale Grosso *Makes 4 servings*

5 pounds kosher salt
1⅔ cups water
8 lemons, thinly sliced
One 3-pound sea bass, gutted and scaled
Salt
¼ cup chopped rosemary

Preheat the oven to 425°F.

In a large bowl, combine the salt with the water. The salt should be moist, not wet. Pack a ½-inch-thick layer of salt in a roasting pan just large enough to hold the fish. Reserve the remaining salt to coat the fish. Place a layer of slightly overlapping lemons over the salt in the pan.

Season the fish, inside and outside, with salt and sprinkle with the fresh rosemary. Place the fish in the lemon-lined roasting pan. Cover the top and sides of the fish with the remaining lemon slices. Pat the remaining salt mixture over the fish to completely enclose it.

Bake until the fish reaches an internal temperature of 150°F on an instant-read thermometer, about 45 minutes. Let cool for 10 minutes, then crack the salt crust with a mallet or hammer. Lift away the salt shell. Discard the lemon and carefully separate the skin from the fish. Transfer portions of the fish fillets to each plate and serve immediately.

MAURIZIO SUGGESTS: For this delicate dish, with its light, lemony taste, I'd suggest a dry white wine with a balanced acidity, such as Pinot Bianco Friulano.

In Venice, we have more sardines in our local waters than we know what to do with. Still, we never tire of new ways to enjoy them. In this refreshing recipe, the sweet-sour flavor of the grapefruit offsets the fried breading and the rich flavor of the sardines. The zest is the secret flavor in the breadcrumbs—when fried, the citrus release its oils and imparts a lovely fragrance. For dressing the salad, consider a peppery Tuscan oil, which holds up against young, bitter greens.

Sardines in Fried Bread with Grapefruit Salad

Sarde Aperte Impanate e Fritte con Insalatina con Pompelmo   *Makes 4 servings*

12 large fresh sardines, each about 6 inches long
   (2 pounds total)
2 pink grapefruit
1 cup mild oil, preferably sunflower
3 large eggs
1 cup all-purpose flour
1 cup unseasoned breadcrumbs (see page 32)
Salt
6 cups baby greens, well rinsed
Extra virgin olive oil for drizzling

To clean the sardines, remove the head, then run your finger from the fish's throat to the rear, scooping out the innards as you pull down with your finger. Thoroughly rinse under cold running water, gently rubbing the scales off the skin; pat dry. Butterfly the sardines, leaving them joined at the back and pulling out the bones with your fingers.

Grate a tablespoon of zest from the grapefruit. Set aside. Section the grapefruit, using a sharp paring knife to remove the peels and all the bitter white pith. Remove the segments from the membrane by sliding the knife on both sides, then lift the segment out. Set aside.

Heat the oil to 340°F in a large heavy skillet set over medium-high heat.

Beat the eggs in a bowl. Add the flour to another bowl and the breadcrumbs with the grapefruit zest to a third. Season the sardines with salt. Dredge them in the flour, gently shaking off the excess, then dip in the egg, followed by the breadcrumbs to coat. Carefully place the breaded sardines into the hot oil, in two batches if necessary to prevent crowding, and cook until golden brown, about 2 minutes. Using tongs or a fork, turn the sardines and brown on the other side, about 2 more minutes. Transfer to a paper towel–lined sheet pan as they cook. Season with salt.

Place a small mound of greens on each serving plate. Arrange the grapefruit sections over the greens, season with salt, and drizzle with olive oil. Place three fried sardines over each salad. Serve immediately.

Squid stewed in its own ink is a specialty of many coastal cuisines, but no one has refined it or made it so much their own as the Venetians. Served over polenta, or stirred into a risotto, its black sauce is visually arresting and compellingly sweet.

Seppie in nero, or "squid in its own ink," in Venice is made with cuttlefish. All cephalopods create ink, which they release to defend themselves against their predators, but cuttlefish produce much more ink and have more delicate flesh than either calamari or octopus.

Black Squid Venetian Style

Seppie in Nero alla Veneziana   *Makes 4 servings*

¼ cup olive oil

2 garlic cloves, crushed

½ small onion, diced

½ celery stalk, diced

1 bay leaf

3 pounds cleaned squid, bodies cut into small triangles,
    tentacles sliced lengthwise

¼ cup dry white wine

Half a 14.5-ounce can peeled whole tomatoes, cut into pieces

1 tablespoon black squid ink

Salt

Heat the olive oil in a medium heavy-bottomed saucepan set over medium heat. Add the garlic, onion, celery, and bay leaf and cook, stirring, until softened, about 5 minutes. Discard the garlic. Add the squid, increase the heat to medium-high, and cook, stirring often, for another 5 minutes. Pour in the wine, and let it evaporate to a couple of tablespoons, then add the tomatoes and some of their juice. Add the black squid ink and season with salt. Lower the heat to a gentle simmer, cover, and cook until the squid is tender and most of the liquid is absorbed, about 50 minutes. Serve immediately with white soft polenta.

MAURIZIO SUGGESTS: The rich, briny taste of squid ink calls for a crisp white wine, such as a Sauvignon Blanc.

Dolci

ON THE WALL OUTSIDE DA FIORE, THE WORDS CALLE DEL SCALETER (STREET OF THE PASTRY COOK) ARE PAINTED IN BLACK AND WHITE. A visitor who's passing by might think nothing of this street sign, but to a Venetian, it's a reminder of one of the sweeter culinary traditions that shaped our city.

This area was full of *scaleteri* during the Renaissance, when sugar was newly traded on the Rialto Bridge and the whole city was indulging its sweet tooth. The *scaleteri* had a famous workshop on our street. Each day they underwent the dangerous task of climbing up the high stairs *(scaleteri)* of the ovens to determine when the baked goods were ready to come out. The *scaleteri* may be long gone, but they are remembered by a sweet biscuit made in the shape of these oven stairs that's sold in local pastry shops today.

Venice has a taste for sweets—gorgeous compositions draped in chocolate, speckled with nuts, powdered with sugar, stuffed with cream, and spiked with grappa. In the old days, the city's penchant for over-the-top celebrations such as Carnevale, and its monopoly on sugar, warranted the production of festive *dolci tipici Veneziani*. In the country, desserts take the shape of comforting, family-style favorites, often made with seasonal fruit and berries. At da Fiore, Mara draws on both city and country traditions.

This smooth pastry cream, a pillar of da Fiore's desserts, is a base to which Mara adds cinnamon, coffee, and sliced fruit and berries, among other flavors. Served as a rich accompaniment to many desserts, they're also divine on their own. There's nothing we love more than dipping a selection of Mara's cookies into little bowls of these flavored creams, chilled or warm.

Pastry Cream

Crema Pasticciera Morbida   *Makes about 2 cups*

1⅔ cups (400 ml) milk
1 vanilla bean, split and scraped, or 1 teaspoon (5 g) pure
   vanilla extract
Zest of ½ lemon, cut into strips
4 large egg yolks
½ cup (100 g) sugar
¼ cup (30 g) all-purpose flour

In a medium, heavy saucepan, combine the milk, vanilla, and lemon zest. Place over medium heat until the milk steams; do not boil. Set aside.

In a medium bowl, beat the yolks and sugar until well combined and slightly pale. Sift the flour into the yolk mixture, beating until smooth. Slowly whisk the hot milk into the egg mixture; do not add it all at once as it may "cook" the eggs. Return the mixture to the saucepan and place over medium heat. Cook, whisking constantly, until the cream boils. Lower the heat and continue cooking (and whisking) until the cream is thick and smooth, about 8 minutes. Transfer to a medium bowl. Chill until cold. This can be made a day in advance.

To make chocolate pastry cream, mix 2 tablespoons good-quality cocoa into the flour and proceed with the recipe. Omit the lemon zest.

To make cinnamon pastry cream, add 2 teaspoons ground cinnamon and 2 cinnamon sticks to the milk and vanilla. Omit the lemon zest. After you incorporate the eggs and prepare the cream, let rest for 15 minutes, then strain through a sieve.

To make coffee cream, reduce the milk by half, replacing it with brewed espresso; omit the lemon zest. Proceed with the recipe.

Light and airy, with hints of lemon, this whipped version is easy to make. We serve it with count-less confections. It will last for two days, covered in your refrigerator.

Whipped Pastry Cream

Crema Pasticciera con Panna   *Makes about 6 cups*

3½ cups (850 ml) milk
1 vanilla bean, split and scraped, or 1 teaspoon (5 g) pure
    vanilla extract
Zest of ½ lemon, cut into strips
8 large egg yolks
1 cup (200 g) sugar
¾ cup (100 g) all-purpose flour
1¼ cups (300 ml) heavy cream

Heat the milk, vanilla, and lemon zest in a medium, heavy saucepan set over medium heat. When the milk steams, remove the pan from the heat. Don't let it boil.

In a medium bowl, beat the yolks and sugar until well combined and slightly pale. Sift the flour into the yolk mixture, beating until smooth. Gradually whisk the hot milk into the egg mixture; do not add all at once or you may "cook" the eggs. Return the mixture to the saucepan and place over medium-low heat. Cook, stirring constantly, until it thickens, 5 to 7 minutes; do not boil. Transfer to a medium bowl and place in an ice bath. Stir often to quickly cool.

Beat the cream to soft peaks in a large bowl. Using a rubber spatula, add the whipped cream to the pasty cream by folding and turning, rather than beating, to incorporate. Cover and chill until ready to use.

Once you learn how to make this classic Marsala-laced custard, dessert can be ready at a moment's notice. *Zabaione,* and its French equivalent, *sabayon,* can be served warm or chilled. Although it's a traditional Venetian filling for cakes and pastries, it's often served on its own, with *baicoli* cookies for spoons. Venetian grooms were presented with a bowl of zabaione, which is famous for its fortifying powers, after they awoke from their first night of married life. *Forza!*

If you love zabaione as much as my family does, consider buying a copper whisking bowl, conically shaped with a rounded bottom. The copper retains steady heat, and the rounded bowl allows you to reach the entire bottom of the pan when stirring. Marsala is readily available in North America, but the custard is just as delicious if you use only the Moscato wine.

Zabaione

Zabaione   *Makes 4 cups*

8 large egg yolks
½ cup (100 g) sugar
½ cup (120 ml) dry Marsala wine
½ cup (120 ml) Moscato wine

Fill the bottom of a double boiler with water to a depth just below the bottom of the insert. Bring the water to a boil over medium-high heat. Reduce the heat to a simmer. In the top of the double boiler, whisk together the yolks, sugar, and wines. Fit the top of the double boiler into the bottom pot and cook the mixture, whisking constantly, until it doubles in volume and the frothy bubbles subside, 5 to 7 minutes. The zabaione is done when a dollop dropped on a plate retains its shape without collapsing. Remove from the heat immediately. Serve warm with Venetian cookies, such as *baicoli,* or chill and serve the next day.

On winter evenings, the spicy fragrance of mulled red wine stewing on home stoves and in local bars wafts into the streets of Venice. In the Veneto, cooks often poach apples in cinnamon- and clove-infused mulled wine and serve them for dessert. We prefer red-tinted pears. Try them with a scoop of vanilla ice cream drizzled with the warm, caramelized reduction of the wine. Kaiser pears, a small Asian variety commonly sold in North American markets, contain firm flesh that holds up well to poaching. The ubiquitous Bosc or Anjou pears, if not overripe, are fine substitutes. We use local Merlot for this dessert, but any dry red table wine is fine.

Pears Poached in Veneto Merlot with Vanilla Gelato

Gelato di Crema con Pere Cotte al Vino Rosso   *Makes 6 servings (about 4 cups)*

Vanilla Gelato
1 lemon
2 cups (480 ml) milk
1 cup (240 ml) heavy cream
3 coffee beans
1 vanilla bean
5 large egg yolks
¾ cup (150 g) sugar

Pears in Veneto Merlot
6 Kaiser pears, or substitute d'Anjou or Bosc if unavailable
2 cups (400 g) sugar
One 750-ml bottle Merlot wine from the Veneto
   or other Merlot
3 cinnamon sticks
2 whole cloves
2 black peppercorns

To make the gelato, using a knife or vegetable peeler, remove the lemon zest in long strips, leaving behind the bitter white pith. Put the lemon zest, milk, cream, and coffee beans into a medium, heavy

saucepan. Split the vanilla bean lengthwise and scrape the seeds into the saucepan, then add the emptied pod. Heat over medium heat, stirring occasionally, until steam rises from the milk; remove from the heat and set aside.

In a medium bowl, beat the yolks and sugar until well combined and slightly pale. Whisk ½ cup of the hot milk/cream mixture into the eggs, then gradually return this custard to the saucepan. Cook over medium-low heat, stirring constantly, until it slightly thickens; do not boil. The ice cream base should be thick enough to coat the back of a spoon. Strain into a medium bowl and discard the lemon zest and vanilla pod. Place the bowl in an ice bath to quickly cool. Transfer to the work bowl of an ice cream maker and churn according to the manufacturer's directions.

To make the pears in Merlot, peel the pears, leaving intact the stem and a small margin of the skin circling it. Using a melon baller, neatly scoop out the bottom core and any visible seeds.

Combine a cup of the sugar, the Merlot, cinnamon sticks, cloves, and peppercorns in a saucepan large enough to hold the pears upright in one layer. Bring the mixture to a boil. Lower the heat to a simmer and, using tongs, place the pears in the pan. Cook, partially covered, until a paring knife easily pierces the base of a pear, about 20 minutes. Remove the pan from the heat and allow the pears to cool in the cooking liquid for 30 minutes to take on more color and flavor.

Transfer the pears to a large plate; set aside.

Add the remaining 1 cup sugar to the cooking liquid and bring to a boil. Cook at a moderate boil until reduced to a thick, caramel-like syrup. Carefully strain the hot syrup through a sieve into a small bowl. Using a paring knife, start at the stem end of the pear and make diagonal incisions down to the base at approximately ½-inch intervals. Place the pear on a serving plate and gently press down on the stem end. The pear will fan out attractively. Generously spoon the wine syrup over the pear. Continue with the remaining pears. Serve with a scoop of the vanilla gelato.

No matter what the season, you can always count on a colorful fruit soup at da Fiore. Mara selects the sweetest, ripest fruit available: apricots in May and June; peaches and plums later in the season; and pears and apples in the fall and early winter. Pineapples carry us through the winter to spring. Mara starts with a 4 to 1 ratio of fruit to sugar (by weight), which creates a not-so-sweet base, and adds more sugar as necessary.

Fruit Soup

Zuppa di Frutta   *Makes 6 servings*

2 pounds fresh apricots or peaches, well washed
1 cup (200 g) sugar
Zest of 1 lemon, cut into strips
1 vanilla bean
Blueberries, raspberries, or strawberries
¼ cup (30 g) slivered almonds
2 tablespoons (4 g) mint leaves, cut into thin ribbons

In a medium saucepan, combine the apricots, sugar, and lemon zest. Split the vanilla bean and, using the side of a paring knife, scrape the seeds and emptied pod into the pan. Add enough cold water to cover the mixture, about 4 cups. Bring to a boil, then lower the heat and simmer for 15 to 20 minutes, or until the fruit is soft but still firm. Remove from the heat; set aside to cool. Discard the lemon zest and vanilla bean. Remove and discard the pits from the apricots. Reserve the cooking liquid. Use a rubber spatula or wooden spoon to work the apricots and 2½ cups of the cooking liquid through a sieve into a bowl. Discard the skins. Alternatively, puree the apricots and the same amount of cooking liquid in a food processor or blender, then work through a sieve for a smooth velvety soup. Cover and refrigerate until well chilled, at least 2 hours.

Ladle the soup into shallow soup bowls and scatter the berries on top. Sprinkle the almonds and mint over the fruit and serve.

Sorbets

Sorbetti

Our freezer is always full of sorbets—there's no better way to refresh the palate after a meal than with these distilled, icy essences of fruit and other flavors.

Like many sweet-toothed children from the Veneto, young Mara and Maurizio used to twist a sweetened licorice stick into a fresh lemon half and then lick it like a lollipop. At da Fiore, we re-create those childhood flavors with a refreshing lemon sorbet topped with tongue-tickling pure grated licorice. It's a more refreshing palate cleanser than the traditional 'sgroppino (a puree of lemon sorbet, vodka, and Prosecco), which is traditionally served at the end of a meal in the Veneto. Pure licorice is sold in 3- to 5-inch pencil-like strips in health and gourmet specialty stores. Grate the licorice on the fine side of a box grater or with a zesting tool.

Lemon Sorbet with Grated Licorice

Sorbetto di Limone e Liquirizia   *Makes 4 to 6 servings*

3 cups (720 ml) fresh lemon juice
1½ cups (450 g) Simple Syrup (page 199)
2 tablespoons (10 g) grated pure licorice

Whisk together the lemon juice and the syrup. Strain through a fine-mesh sieve. Discard the lemon seeds; reserve the liquid and any pulp in a large bowl. Freeze in an ice cream maker according to the manufacturer's instructions.

In our local dialect, *ratafia'* means "to breathe again," and it's the name of a strong coffee liqueur that's popular for its potent caffeine kick. The tradition stems from Murano, where glassmakers used to sip this rejuvenating liqueur to keep warm during breaks. This sorbet is made with regular coffee, but if you prefer an even stronger taste, add up to two extra shots of espresso.

Turkish-Style Espresso Sorbet

Ratafia' Sorbetto di Caffè   *Makes 4 servings*

3 cups (720 ml) water
2 cups (175 g) ground espresso beans
1 cup (240 ml) Simple Syrup (page 199)
7 tablespoons (100 ml) dark rum
1 cup (240 ml) light whipping cream
12 whole espresso beans to garnish

In a small saucepan, bring the water to a boil and add a third of the ground espresso. Remove from the heat, stir and set aside for a moment or two. Bring the mixture to a boil again and stir in another third of the espresso. Remove from heat for another moment, then repeat with the remaining espresso. Set aside to cool for 10 minutes.

Using a ladle, remove the brewed coffee from the top, taking care not to disturb the grounds resting on the bottom of the saucepan; leave up to half an inch of coffee behind in the pan. Discard the grounds. Strain the prepared coffee through a fine-mesh sieve into a large bowl and stir in the syrup and the rum. Chill for an hour. Transfer the mixture to an ice cream maker, then freeze according to the manufacturer's instructions. To serve, portion in glass or ceramic dessert cups and pour ¼ cup cream over the top and around the sides of each serving. Garnish each serving with three espresso beans and serve.

Venetians are particularly fond of this sweet, red strawberry grape, an American variety that was brought to Venice around the turn of the last century. The regional dessert wine made from these grapes tastes of concentrated strawberries—hence its name, *fragolino,* Italian for strawberry. But while strawberry grapes have enjoyed immense popularity in the Veneto for more than a century, they've all but disappeared in the United States. When testing grape varieties for this recipe, we found that the small, seedless red grapes available in North American groceries produce similar results.

Strawberry Grape Sorbet

Sorbetto di Uva Fragola   *Makes 6 to 8 servings*

6 cups (1 kg) chilled strawberry grapes, or red seedless grapes
¾ cup (180 ml) Simple Syrup (recipe follows)

Pass the strawberry grapes through a sieve into a medium bowl, working the mixture with a rubber spatula or pastry scraper until only seeds and skins remain in the sieve. Add half the syrup to the bowl; taste for sweetness. Add more syrup if necessary; stir to combine. Transfer the mixture to an ice cream maker, then freeze according to the manufacturer's instructions.

This syrup will last in the refrigerator for up to a week.

Simple Syrup   *Makes 4 cups*

3 cups (720 ml) water
3½ cups (840 ml) sugar

Combine the water and sugar in a 2-quart heavy saucepan and place over medium-high heat. Bring the mixture to a boil, then simmer, stirring occasionally, until the syrup thickens slightly, about 20 minutes. Remove from the heat and set aside to cool. Cover and chill until ready for use.

In the countryside where Mara and Maurizio grew up, rustic farm-style desserts like this one are popular. Mara's "crown" of apples and pastry is an updated strudel with the addition of pine nuts and lemon zest. When served hot and drizzled with a sweet cinnamon cream, it's one of our favorite winter treats. Though we make our own pastry at the restaurant, high-quality, store-bought frozen puff pastry, such as Pepperidge Farms, works just as well.

Apple Crown with Raisins and Cinnamon Pastry Cream

Corona di Mele e Uvetta con Crema Profumata alla Cannella   *Makes 8 to 10 servings*

¾ cup (100 g) seedless raisins

4 tablespoons (60 ml) grappa

¼ pound (1 stick) (120 g) plus 1 tablespoon (5 g) unsalted
    butter, at room temperature

¼ cup (30 g) all-purpose flour for dusting

2 medium apples (300 g), peeled, cored, and cubed

1⅓ cups (250 g) sugar

6 tablespoons (90 ml) water

2 teaspoons grated lemon zest

1 teaspoon (2 g) ground cinnamon

One 17.3-ounce package puff pastry, defrosted as directed on
    package

⅓ cup (50 g) pine nuts

1 large egg, lightly beaten

1 recipe warm Cinnamon Pastry Cream (page 188)

Place the raisins in a small bowl. Cover with 3 tablespoons of the grappa. Set aside for at least an hour.

Using a tablespoon of the butter, thoroughly coat an 18 × 12-inch baking sheet. Dust with ⅛ cup of the flour, shaking off any excess. Set aside.

Combine the apples, ⅔ cup of the sugar, the water, lemon zest, and ½ teaspoon cinnamon in a medium saucepan. Bring to a boil, then lower the heat and cook, stirring often, until the apples are very soft, about 10 minutes. Add the remaining 1 tablespoon grappa and cook, stirring often, to reduce to a thick applesauce consistency; make sure that the mixture is smooth and all excess liquid has evaporated. Set aside to cool.

In a standing mixer, beat the remaining butter and sugar together until pale and creamy. Stir in the remaining ½ teaspoon cinnamon. Set aside.

Use the remaining flour to lightly dust a clean work surface. Roll the puff pastry into an approximately 18 × 14-inch rectangle; the dough should be ⅛ inch thick. Use a knife to trim the edges. Using a spatula, spread the butter and sugar mixture on the dough, leaving a ½-inch margin all around. Drain the raisins and sprinkle them over the dough. Spread the apple mixture over the raisins and sprinkle with pine nuts.

With a long side facing you, roll the dough away from you into a tight, neat cylinder. Transfer the cylinder to the prepared baking pan. Take one end in each hand and bring the ends together, gently pressing to join them and form a ring. Using a sharp paring knife, make slits about an inch apart, starting about ½ inch from the interior edge of the ring. These slits will separate further, forming decorative V shapes as the pastry cooks. Transfer the pastry ring to the refrigerator to "rest" for 15 minutes.

While the pastry rests, preheat the oven to 475°F.

In a small bowl, beat the egg with a tablespoon of water. Using a pastry brush, lightly coat the dough with the egg wash. Transfer the pan to the oven and bake for 2 minutes, then lower the temperature to 375°F and bake for another 30 minutes, or until golden. Remove the pan from the oven and let cool. If serving immediately, transfer the *corona* to a serving platter and spoon the warm cinnamon cream into the center. Serve immediately.

MAURIZIO SUGGESTS: Recioto di Soave Passito, with its woody, spicy, full-bodied flavor, is an extraordinary accompaniment.

Sweetened with fresh, dried, and candied fruits and spiked with grappa, this is our version of pinza, the traditional polenta cake that Venetians enjoy on Epiphany every January 5 and 6. Variations of this *dolce dei poveri,* or dessert of the poor, exist in every corner of our region—some areas make it with soaked day-old bread or semolina rather than polenta; others serve it more as a snack than a sweet dessert; and still others sweeten it the old-fashioned way, with honey. One thing is sure—everyone claims that his grandmother's version is the best! We add potent intrigue to this otherwise simple pleasure by plumping up the raisins with grappa and water first. If you don't have this fiery spirit on hand, substitute rum.

Fruit-Filled Polenta Cake

Pinza Alla Veneziana *Makes 12 servings*

¾ cup (100 g) seedless raisins
½ cup (120 ml) grappa plus 3 tablespoons (50 ml)
 for soaking raisins
4 tablespoons (½ stick) (60 g) unsalted butter,
 at room temperature
¼ cup (10 g) finely ground fresh breadcrumbs
1¾ cups (240 g) coarsely ground yellow cornmeal
1 cup (120 g) all-purpose flour
5 cups (1200 ml) milk
1⅓ cups (250 g) sugar
2 tablespoons (30 ml) olive oil
Pinch salt
4 large eggs
1 teaspoon (5 g) pure vanilla extract
1 tablespoon (10 g) baking powder
1 cup (200 g) sliced dried figs
1 large apple (200 g), peeled, cored, and diced
⅓ cup (50 g) pine nuts
⅓ cup (50 g) chopped candied orange
1 tablespoon (6 g) fennel seeds
Confectioners' sugar for dusting (optional)

Place the raisins in a small bowl. Cover with the 3 tablespoons grappa and add enough water to completely cover the raisins. Set aside for at least an hour.

Preheat the oven to 350°F. Lightly grease a 12-inch springform pan with a tablespoon of the butter. Add the breadcrumbs, turning the pan to coat; gently tap out any excess. Set aside.

In a medium bowl, mix together the cornmeal and the flour. Set aside.

In a medium saucepan, combine the milk, sugar, oil, salt, and the remaining 3 tablespoons butter and place over medium heat. When the mixture steams just prior to a boil, pour in the flour mixture in a steady stream, whisking constantly. Reduce the temperature to low and cook, whisking frequently, until the mixture is of a thick polenta-like consistency and pulls away from the sides of the pan, about 10 minutes. Remove the pan from the heat and stir in the ½ cup grappa. Beat the eggs into the polenta one by one, fully incorporating with each addition. Stir in the vanilla and baking powder.

Drain the raisins, discarding the grappa. Stir the raisins, figs, apple, pine nuts, and candied orange into the batter. Using a spatula and dipping it into water with each stroke, spread the batter into the prepared springform pan. Sprinkle the top with fennel seeds. Bake for 50 minutes, or until the dough pulls away from the sides of the pan. Cool for 5 minutes on a rack, then release the spring and remove the sides. Cool. Serve slices topped with confectioners' sugar, if using.

Though this is nothing like the Treviso-born tiramisù popularized across the world, we've christened it with the same name because it's just as much a "pick-me-up." The hazelnut cookies soak up the sweet vermouth and are layered with the creamy, whipped mascarpone. Since no cooking is necessary, it is perfect for summer entertaining. The diameter of amaretti cookies varies from brand to brand: two 7-ounce packages of approximately 2-inch amaretti cookies will provide three layers in a 9-inch dish. If you choose to serve this in little individual dessert bowls as we do, purchase the "mini" amaretti. Or make your own (page 227)!

Tiramisù Venetian Style

Dolce all'Amaretto   *Makes 8 servings*

6 large eggs, separated
4 tablespoons (50 g) sugar
2 cups (500 g) mascarpone cheese, drained of any excess
    liquid
1 cup (240 ml) sweet vermouth
Two 7-ounce (420 g) packages amaretti cookies

In a medium bowl, beat the egg yolks with 3 tablespoons of the sugar until foamy and pale. Beat in the mascarpone until smooth. Stir in the egg yolks; set aside.

In a large bowl, using a standing or hand-held mixer, whip the egg whites until frothy. Add the remaining tablespoon of sugar and beat until they hold stiff peaks. Fold the mascarpone mixture into the egg whites. Set aside.

Pour the vermouth into a small bowl. Reserve five amaretti cookies to crumble and sprinkle over the top of the dessert. One at a time, dip the remaining amaretti cookies into the vermouth; they should absorb some of the liquid but not be mushy. Place the soaked amaretti in one snug layer on the bottom of a 9-inch ceramic dish or pie plate. Evenly spread half of the mascarpone mixture over the amaretti. Place another layer of soaked cookies over the mascarpone. Repeat the layering, spreading the remaining mascarpone mixture, then ending with a layer of soaked cookies; this layer should be loosely arranged so that the cream mixture below is visible. Sprinkle with the crumbled dry amaretti. Refrigerate to set for at least 2 hours.

With luscious molten chocolate hidden inside intensely rich exteriors, the whole set atop plates of coffee cream, these individual cakes are, without a doubt, our most sensual desserts. Mara tested this recipe for two years, tweaking and improving until she finally achieved the perfect consistency both inside and out. Use the best chocolate you can find: We use Callebaut, but Valrhona, Scharffen Berger, or Ghirardelli work very well. The chocolate must contain at least 75 percent cacao (it will say so on the package), or this recipe won't work.

This recipe is a host's dream. It is a cinch to prepare—you can make the cake batter and fill the ramekins a day or two in advance and keep them covered in your refrigerator. Since the inside chocolate must be soft and at room temperature before being placed in the oven, take the ramekins out of the refrigerator at least an hour before cooking.

Warm Chocolate Cake da Fiore

Tortino di Ciocolato   *Makes six 4-ounce ramekins*

6 tablespoons (90 g) unsalted butter plus more to butter molds
1½ tablespoons (15 g) all-purpose flour plus 2 tablespoons
   (15 g) to dust molds
5 ounces (150 g) good-quality chocolate, broken in small
   chunks
2 tablespoons (30 ml) rum
3 large eggs, separated
¼ cup (50 g) sugar
Confectioners' sugar for dusting
½ recipe Coffee Cream (recipe follows)
6 fresh raspberries

Lightly coat six 4-ounce ramekins or soufflé molds with butter. Dust with the 2 tablespoons flour, rolling the ramekins to evenly coat; lightly tap out any excess. Set aside.

Fill the bottom of a double boiler with water to a depth just below but not touching the top insert. Bring the water to a boil. Place the chocolate, rum, and the remaining butter in the top of the double boiler and insert over the gently boiling water. Cook, stirring often, until the chocolate is completely melted. Remove from the heat and let cool almost to room temperature.

Preheat the oven to 400°F.

Transfer the egg whites to the work bowl of a standing mixer or keep them in a mixing bowl and, using a hand-held mixer, beat on high speed until they hold stiff peaks. Reduce the speed to low and add the sugar, egg yolks, and the remaining 1½ tablespoons flour; mix just until fully incorporated. Remove the bowl from the standing mixer, if using, and, with a rubber spatula, fold in the chocolate mixture. Divide the chocolate among the prepared ramekins, filling each three-quarters full. Bake for 8 to 10 minutes or until a slight crack appears in the top of each cake. Gently turn each ramekin upside down over a serving plate to invert the cake. Serve dusted with confectioners' sugar and a small pool of coffee cream. Garnish with a fresh raspberry, if using.

Serve alongside the outrageously rich Tortino, or enjoy it on its own with a selection of cookies.

Coffee Cream

Crema di Caffè   *Makes about 4 cups*

2 cups (480 ml) espresso or brewed coffee
2 cups (480 ml) milk
8 large egg yolks
1 cup (200 g) sugar
1 teaspoon (5 g) pure vanilla extract
4 tablespoons (30 g) all-purpose flour

Combine the espresso and the milk in a small saucepan and place over medium heat. When steam rises from the mixture, remove the pan from the heat. Set aside.

In a small bowl, beat the eggs, sugar, and vanilla. Add the flour; stir to combine. Beat a few tablespoons of the hot milk and espresso mixture into this, then gradually stir this mixture into the saucepan. Cook over medium-low heat, stirring almost constantly, until the mixture thickens. The cream should coat the back of a spoon and hold the outline of your finger after you pass it through. Strain the custard into a bowl. Place in an ice bath to cool quickly, then cover and refrigerate. Use within 2 days.

MAURIZIO SUGGESTS: A sweet, full-bodied red wine, such as Barolo Chinato, pairs beautifully, especially when served cold.

This wintry chestnut custard is Maurizio's favorite. The rich attributes of the chestnut are at their best here, whipped into a deceptively light eggless cream. Although it is spectacular on its own, we pair it with a succulent sauce made from ripe persimmons, which are as plentiful as the chestnuts in the Veneto at the same time of the year. The best kind to use are the round, squat specimens known as Kaki Vanille that are exported from Italy to North America. The Asian-imported Hachiya make for a somewhat tarter substitute.

Chestnut Mousse with Persimmon Sauce

Mousse di Castagne   *Makes 6 to 8 servings*

1 pound (450 g) fresh chestnuts (substitute 10 ounces [300 g] frozen, peeled chestnuts)
2 cups (480 ml) milk
1½ cups (360 ml) Simple Syrup (page 199)
2 tablespoons (60 g) cocoa powder
2 envelopes (8 g) unflavored gelatin
2 cups (480 ml) heavy cream
1 recipe Persimmon Sauce (recipe follows)
Chestnut flour to garnish (optional)

To prepare the chestnuts, using a sharp paring knife, make a lengthwise incision on their curved side. Place them in a bowl and cover with cold water. Set aside for 2 hours.

Preheat the oven to 350°F.

Drain the chestnuts and place in a roasting pan (use two pans, if necessary, to hold them in one layer). Roast until they split open and are well browned, about 50 minutes. When they are cool enough to handle, peel away and discard the shell and outer skin. Prepare the chestnuts up to a day in advance.

Put the peeled chestnuts in a medium saucepan and add the milk.

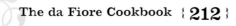

Add the syrup and place over medium heat. When the milk steams, remove it from the heat. Stir in the cocoa. Transfer the chestnut mixture to a food processor and process until smooth. Transfer to a large bowl. Set aside.

In a small bowl, soften the gelatin in ½ cup water for 10 minutes. Drain the gelatin and transfer to a small saucepan. Heat over low heat just until the gelatin dissolves, stirring constantly (about a minute). Remove from the heat and set aside briefly to cool slightly. Mix the gelatin into the chestnut mixture. Refrigerate or place the bowl in an ice bath to quickly cool; it should be cool, but not cold. Stir occasionally to hasten chilling.

Whip the cream until it holds soft peaks, then fold into the chestnuts. Cover and refrigerate until ready to serve. The dessert can be prepared to this point up to a day in advance.

To serve, spoon a small pool of persimmon sauce on one side of each serving plate. Using an oval ice cream scoop, place three scoops of chestnut mousse in the center of each dessert plate. Rest a fourth scoop on top of the others. Place the chestnut flour, if using, in a fine-mesh strainer and sprinkle a little over each mound of mousse.

Persimmon Sauce

Crema di Kaki   *Makes 6 to 8 servings*

5 ripe persimmons
⅓ to ½ cup (80 to 120 ml) Simple Syrup (page 199)
1 tablespoon anise liqueur (optional)

Remove the stem caps from the persimmons and scoop the soft, orange flesh into a sieve. With a wooden spoon, press the flesh through the sieve into a bowl. Whisk in the syrup, tasting to adjust the amount to the sweetness of the fruit. Stir in the anise. Chill until ready to serve.

Some sweets are so rich, so decadent, and so over-the-top that you can't help feeling a little guilty when it's all over. Our *crema fritta,* deep-fried custard squares covered in confectioners' sugar and topped with fresh whipped cream, is one of them. This traditional recipe calls for *rosolio,* a liqueur made from rose petals that families in the Veneto often bottle themselves—its light, flowery flavor adds delicious intrigue to the custard. If you can't find Rosolio (you likely won't unless you bring a bottle back in your suitcase), Cointreau is a fine substitute.

Venetian Fried Cream

Crema Fritta alla Veneziana   *Makes 6 servings*

1 quart (1 liter) milk
¼ cup (60 ml) Rosolio or Cointreau plus 1 cup (240 ml)
    Rosolio, or water, for dipping
Grated zest of 1 lemon
1 vanilla bean, split and scraped, or 1 teaspoon (5 g) vanilla
    extract
8 large egg yolks
6 large eggs
1⅓ cups (250 g) sugar
2 cups (250 g) all-purpose flour
4 tablespoons (1/2 stick) (60 g) unsalted butter, at room
    temperature

1 quart (1 liter) sunflower, safflower or corn oil
Grated zest of 1 lemon
1 cup (125 g) all-purpose flour
2 cups (90 g) finely ground fresh breadcrumbs
3 cups (180 g) heavy cream, whipped
Confectioners' sugar for dusting

Line a 13 × 9 × 1-inch deep baking pan with parchment paper. Lightly spray or coat the surface with oil or butter. Set aside.

Heat the milk, the ¼ cup Rosolio or Cointreau, the lemon zest, and vanilla in a medium, heavy saucepan set over medium heat. When the milk steams, remove it from the heat.

In a medium bowl, beat the egg yolks and four of the eggs with the sugar until slightly pale and thickened. Sift the flour into the egg mixture and beat until smooth. Beat in the butter. Add the hot milk, stirring constantly until well combined. Return the mixture to the saucepan and place over medium heat. Cook, stirring constantly, until the mixture is thickened, almost a polenta consistency, about 10 minutes. Transfer to the prepared baking pan and, using a spatula, spread evenly; dip the spatula in Rosolio or cold water between strokes to prevent sticking (reserve the Rosolio, if using). Let cool, then transfer to the refrigerator to chill and set for at least 4 hours.

Cut the chilled cream into three even, lengthwise columns, 3 inches each, and into 4 rows, about 3¼ inches each; dip the knife into the Rosolio or cold water between cuts to prevent sticking. Using a circular pastry cutter, you may also cut decorative circles; however, there is more waste in doing so.

Line a baking sheet with paper towels.

In a large Dutch oven, heat the sunflower oil over medium-high heat to 350°F. In a medium bowl, beat the remaining eggs with the lemon zest. One by one, remove the cream squares from the baking pan, dredge in the flour, then dip in the eggs and dredge in the breadcrumbs, gently pressing the crumbs onto the firm cream. Place the cream squares, one by one, into the hot oil; do not crowd the pan. Fry until golden on the bottom, about 2 minutes. Using tongs or a spatula, turn the cream over and cook for another 2 minutes. Transfer the fried cream to the paper towel–lined baking sheet as they brown. Place two squares of fried cream on each plate, along with a generous dollop of whipped cream. Sprinkle the fried cream with confectioners' sugar and serve.

Mara's aunt was famous for her sweet, chewy apple focaccia, which she prepared every autumn. Our favorite version calls for ripe summer figs, but the rest of the year, we replace the same amount of fruit with whatever is in season—pears, berries, and cherries all yield spectacular results. Make it ahead; it will last for two to three days in a tightly sealed container.

Sweet Focaccia with Figs

Focaccia di Fichi   *Makes 10 servings*

10 tablespoons (1¼ sticks) (180 g) unsalted butter, heated
    until almost liquid, plus some for buttering the pan
2⅓ cups (300 g) all-purpose flour plus some for dusting
    the pan
1 teaspoon (4 g) dry yeast
½ cup (120 ml) warm milk
4 large eggs
1½ cups (300 g) sugar
1½ pounds (675 g) fresh figs, peeled and quartered lengthwise
1 recipe Pastry Cream (page 188)
Confectioners' sugar for dusting

Preheat the oven to 350°F. Lightly butter the sides of a 12-inch springform pan and sift a couple of tablespoons of flour into the pan; invert to remove excess flour. Set aside.

In a small bowl, mix the yeast into the milk. Set aside until frothy.

In a large bowl, beat the eggs and the sugar. Beat in the 10 tablespoons butter. Add half the flour, followed by the milk. When well combined, mix in the remaining flour to form a soft dough. Evenly spread three-quarters of the dough into the prepared pan. Place the figs evenly over the top, then heap generous spoonfuls of the remaining dough around the top. Bake until golden and firm, 50 to 55 minutes. Cool on a rack for 5 minutes, then release the spring on the springform pan. Serve in wedges at room temperature dusted with confectioners' sugar and a spoonful of pastry cream.

Carnevale wouldn't be the same without these crisp, chewy, sugar-sprinkled fritters, which are consumed throughout the feast days. The tradition dates back hundreds of years, and countless generations of cooks have added all kinds of sweet and savory fillings. After a meal at da Fiore, we don't expect our guests to have room for anything so rich, so Mara developed this lighter version fragranced with citrus zest. The potato flour gives the dough an airy texture.

Sweet Carnival Fritters

Le Frittelle di Carnevale　　*Makes about 42 fritters*

⅓ cup (50 g) raisins
4 tablespoons (60 ml) rum
1½ cups (185 g) all-purpose flour
¼ cup (45 g) potato flour
1⅓ cups (320 ml) water
¼ cup (50 g) sugar
4 tablespoons (½ stick) (60 g) unsalted butter
1 teaspoon (5 g) pure vanilla extract
Pinch salt
4 large eggs
Grated zest of ½ lemon
Grated zest of ½ orange
1 teaspoon (4 g) baking powder
2 quarts (2 liters) corn, sunflower, or safflower oil
Confectioners' sugar for dusting

Combine the raisins, 2 tablespoons of the rum, and just enough warm water to cover in a small bowl and let stand for 2 hours to macerate.

In a medium bowl, combine the all-purpose and potato flours. Set aside.

In a medium saucepan, put the water, sugar, butter, vanilla, salt, and the remaining 2 tablespoons rum. Bring the mixture to a boil. Lower the heat and stir in the flour mixture to form a ball of dough; cook, stirring constantly, for 2 to 3 minutes. Transfer the hot dough to the work bowl of a standing mixer fitted with the paddle attachment. On low speed, work the dough to cool it slightly. Add the eggs, one at a time; completely incorporate each egg between additions. Increase the speed of the mixer as necessary. Add the lemon and orange zests and the baking powder. Drain the raisins and mix them into the dough. The consistency of the dough should be soft and slightly sticky.

Heat the oil in a large Dutch oven or heavy pot to 350°F. Use a teaspoon to scoop a ball of dough and, using your finger, push it off the spoon into the hot oil. Repeat, filling the Dutch oven with one layer of dough balls; depending on the size of the Dutch oven, about three batches will be necessary, so do not crowd. The addition of dough will lower the temperature; adjust the heat as necessary to maintain a constant temperature of the oil. Fry the dough, turning with tongs or a fork here and there, until they are evenly golden, 3 to 4 minutes. Transfer the fritters to a paper towel–lined sheet pan as they cook. To serve, arrange the fritters on a decorative platter and dust with confectioners' sugar.

Carnevale

CARNEVALE, WHICH TRANSLATES LITERALLY as "meat is allowed," is the last hurrah before the abstemious period of Lent. Each year, our streets swell with thousands of visitors and Venetians who parade through town in costume, reveling in the festivities. We celebrate Carnevale with the same strain of sweet, fried goodness you find at street fairs all over the world. *Le Fritelle,* the fried dough sprinkled with confectioners' sugar, and *galani,* otherwise known as *crostoli,* the long strips of fried, sweetened dough, are two of our favorites.

In Venice, they're called *ga'lani;* in Trentino, *crostoli;* in Tuscany, *cenci*—these light, crisp, fried dough treats are a staple Italian pastry. Ours are named for the long, twisted *gala,* which means ribbons. In Venice, the tradition dates back to the 1500s, when they were called *"fritelle piene di Vento,"* or fritters full of wind, for the crackly air bubbles that make them so much fun to eat. They're often made with grappa, but we grew up making them with rum—a country twist that yields a sweeter cookie. Naturally, we're partial to our family recipe.

Galani

Ga'lani   *Makes about 60*

2 large eggs
2 tablespoons (25 g) sugar
Pinch salt
2 tablespoons (30 ml) olive oil
2 tablespoons (30 ml) rum
½ teaspoon (2 g) pure vanilla extract
Grated zest of ½ lemon
2 cups (250 g) all-purpose flour
1 teaspoon (4 g) baking powder
2 quarts (2 liters) corn, sunflower, or safflower oil
Confectioners' sugar for dusting

In a large bowl, beat together the eggs, sugar, and salt. Whisk in the oil, then the rum, vanilla, and lemon zest. Using a wooden spoon, mix in the flour and baking powder. Once the dough comes together, turn it out onto a work surface lightly dusted with flour and knead until it is smooth and uniform; continue to dust with flour as necessary to prevent sticking. Place in a bowl, cover, and set aside for 3 hours to relax the dough.

Cut the dough into quarters and roll them through a pasta machine, one by one, until you reach the finest setting. Dust the sheets of dough as necessary to prevent sticking and cut the pasta sheets to keep them at rectangles of manageable size as they pass through the finer settings of the machine.

Using a scalloped-edged pastry cutter, trim each rectangular sheet of dough to make it even. Use the cutter to cut 3-inch-wide horizontal strips of dough. Roll the pastry cutter in the middle of the bottom, center, and top of each strip, taking care not to cut over to the edges; the slashes will help the oil penetrate the inside of the dough, resulting in a well puffed galani.

Heat the oil in a large Dutch oven or heavy pot to 350°F. Place just enough strips of dough into the hot oil to fit without crowding. Fry until golden and puffed, turning them once during cooking, 30 to 40 seconds per side. Transfer the galani to a paper towel–lined sheet pan as they cook. To serve, mound the galani on a platter and dust with confectioners' sugar.

Venetian Cookies

Biscotti e Biscottini

Five o'clock is cookie hour in Venice. Traditionally, this time of day was reserved for dipping biscotti into *rosolio*, a liqueur made out of rose petals. Sweet and aromatic dessert wines, such as recioto di Soave passito or Moscato d'Asti, are often biscotti partners during this afternoon snack. Many of these cookies contain grappa, whose pronounced potency softens with cooking and functions as a vehicle for other flavors. If you don't have grappa, substitute rum.

There's one cookie that Venetians always have in the house, but for the most part, they are store bought—the venerable *baicoli*. These dense, thin, oval biscuits have a mild flavor that's a bit saltier than it is sweet. They're the most popular choice for dipping into sweet wine, zabaione, and all of the flavored custards enjoyed at the end of the meal. Believed to date back to the seventeenth century, *baicoli* were prized for their long shelf life. Indeed, as a result of the multiple bakings that concentrate their flavor and reduce moisture, these cookies will last for years without spoiling. The laborious cooking also explains why Venetians are more than happy with high-quality artisanal *baicoli* available at bakeries across town.

At the end of each meal, Maurizio delivers a little plate full of Mara's biscotti to bid our guests good-bye. The recipes listed below are made in miniature for this farewell gesture—tiny amaretti, minuscule meringues, and bite-sized galani—a Venetian way of extending the pleasures of the table for a few more sweet moments.

Meringues—sugar and egg whites whisked together and slow-baked into crisp cookies like this one—have a special place at the Venetian dessert table. Crunchy, crumbly, and sweet, two meringues are often stuck together with a center of dark, melted chocolate.

Meringues with Sliced Almonds

Meringhe con Le Mandorle   *Makes about 5 dozen*

8 large egg whites
3 cups (600 g) sugar
1½ cups (180 g) slivered almonds

Preheat the oven to 200°F.

Line two baking sheets with parchment paper. Set aside.

Fill a large saucepan three-quarters full with water. Bring to a boil, then lower the heat to a simmer. Combine the egg whites and the sugar in a large bowl. Place the bowl atop the simmering water and whisk aggressively until the egg whites are foamy and the sugar has completely dissolved, about 10 minutes.

Transfer the egg whites to the work bowl of a standing mixer, or keep them in the bowl and use a hand-held mixer to beat on high speed until they are glossy and sticky.

Transfer the meringue mixture to a pastry bag fitted with a smooth tip (about an inch in diameter). Using a circular motion, squeeze the meringue into 1½- to 2-inch circles about 1 inch apart on the parchment-lined baking sheets. Piping the meringue in a circular motion with a pointed top creates an attractive and lighter meringue. Sprinkle the almonds over the meringues. Bake for 3 hours until completely dried. Remove the meringue to wire racks to cool. The meringues can be stored in an airtight container at room temperature for up to five days.

Mara found this recipe in an old Venetian cookbook and adapted it to make these little lovely cookies topped with toasted hazelnuts. These eggless sweets are faintly fragrant with grappa and crunchy to the core.

Hazelnut Cookies

Grappini alle Nocciole   *Makes about 3 dozen*

1¾ cups (220 g) all-purpose flour
1 cup (120 g) chopped skinned hazelnuts plus 36 whole
    hazelnuts
½ cup (100 g) sugar
Pinch salt
Grated zest of ½ lemon
¼ pound (1 stick) (120 g) unsalted butter, at room
    temperature, cut into pieces
⅓ cup (80 ml) grappa (substitute rum)

Preheat the oven to 350°F. Line two baking sheets with parchment paper.

In a large bowl, combine the flour, chopped hazelnuts, sugar, salt, and lemon zest. Pour the dry mixture onto a flat work surface. Using your hands, scatter pieces of the softened butter over the mixture and pour in the grappa. Knead the mixture together to make a smooth dough.

Pull off small pieces of the dough (about ¾ ounce) and roll into small balls, about 1½ inches in diameter, and place on the prepared baking sheets. Using the thumb and index finger of both hands, pinch the centers of the balls together to make an impression like a four-leaf clover. Place a whole hazelnut in the center and gently press the dough around it to seal it in place. Bake the cookies until golden brown, about 15 minutes. Cool for 2 minutes on the sheet before using a spatula to transfer to a wire rack to cool. Store in a tightly covered container for up to 2 weeks.

Everyone has a favorite recipe for traditional amaretti; ours comes from a friend of Mara's grand-mother. It couldn't be simpler: hazelnuts, almonds, egg whites, and sugar, puffed up into airy, crunchy bites. They bake very quickly, but the batter has to refrigerate for twelve hours or the cookies will be too soft.

Amaretto Cookies

Amaretti   *Makes about 4 dozen*

2 cups (250g) chopped hazelnuts
2 cups (250 g) chopped almonds
2⅓ cups (450 g) sugar
6 large egg whites

In a large bowl, stir together the hazelnuts, almonds, and a cup of the sugar. Add the egg whites, mixing until all of the ingredients are incorporated; the dough will be sticky. Cover and refrigerate for 12 hours, or until the dough is firm and easy to work with.

Preheat the oven to 350°F. Line two baking sheets with parchment paper.

Spread the remaining 1⅓ cups sugar in a small baking pan. Using a small ice cream scoop or 2 teaspoons, scoop small balls of the dough and drop them into the sugar. Shake the pan to turn the dough balls and evenly coat with the sugar. Place on the prepared baking sheets about 2 inches apart. Bake until golden brown, 12 to 15 minutes. Cool for 2 minutes on the sheet before using a spatula to transfer to a rack to cool. Store in an airtight container for up to 2 weeks.

MAURIZIO SUGGESTS: An Asti spumante, preferably a *metodo classico* from Monferrato, is delicious paired with amaretti. The bubbles enliven the palate after each rich bite.

This crumbly, buttery, lemon-scented ring is the quintessential Venetian cookie. Also known as *buranelli* (since they hail from the island of Burano), each one has a *buco*, or hole in the center, called a *buso* in Venetian. They're an all-purpose cookie, equally good with a cup of tea or a glass of milk. Since their texture allows them to soak up liquid like a sponge, bakers began making *esse*, S-shaped cookies which are easier to dip. These are made in the traditional ring shape.

Venetian Bussolai

Bussolai alla Veneziana   *Makes about 4 dozen*

1⅓ cups (175 g) all-purpose flour
½ cup (100 g) sugar
5 large egg yolks
½ teaspoon (2 g) pure vanilla extract
Grated zest of ½ lemon
6 tablespoons (90 g) unsalted butter, at room temperature

Mound the flour and sugar on a large work surface. Using your hands, stir the ingredients together. Hollow out a center well, leaving an outside ring of the flour and sugar mixture. Put the yolks, vanilla, and lemon zest inside the ring and place pieces of the butter along the flour rim. Using your hands, slowly incorporate the flour mixture into the eggs, then work the ingredients together, kneading the dough for 5 minutes.

Preheat the oven to 350°F. Line two baking sheets with parchment paper.

Divide the dough in quarters and roll into balls slightly smaller than tennis balls. On a surface lightly dusted with flour roll each ball into a ½-inch-thick log. Cut the log into 4-inch segments. Bring the two tips together to form a ring, or circle with a center hole, and place the circles on the prepared baking sheet about an inch apart. Bake until lightly browned on the edges and bottom, 12 to 14 minutes. Cool for 2 minutes on the sheet before using a spatula to transfer to a rack to cool. Store in an airtight container for up to 2 weeks.

These crunchy little almond horns were inspired by an eggless cookie recipe that Mara stumbled on twenty years ago in an old Austrian cookbook. They're now a regular feature on our winter biscottini platter.

Half-Moon Almond Cookies

Cornetti alle Mandorle   *Makes about 4 dozen*

2 cups (250 g) all-purpose flour
½ cup (100 g) sugar
¾ cup (100 g) chopped almonds
Pinch salt
14 tablespoons (1¾ sticks) (200 g) unsalted butter, at room
    temperature, divided into small pieces
Confectioners' sugar for dusting

In a medium bowl, mix together the flour, sugar, almonds, and salt. Pour the dry mixture onto a flat work surface. Using your hands, scatter pieces of the butter over the mound of flour. Work the mixture together, kneading it until the dough is just smooth and uniform. Wrap in plastic wrap and refrigerate for at least 30 minutes, or up to 2 days.

Preheat the oven to 350°F. Line two baking sheets with parchment paper.

Pinch off a small amount of the dough, about ½ ounce or the size of a large olive, and roll it into a 4-inch log. Bend the ends of the log toward one another to form a crescent shape. Repeat with the remaining dough, placing the shaped cookies on the prepared baking sheet approximately an inch apart. Bake until lightly browned, 12 to 15 minutes. Cool for 2 minutes on the sheet before using a spatula to transfer to a rack to cool. Store, tightly covered, for up to a month. Sprinkle with confectioners' sugar before serving.

These crumbly, oval butter cookies are named after their yellow color—*zalo* in the Venetian dialect—since they're made with yellow polenta. If you like, liberally dust them with confectioners' sugar before serving, as we do.

Cornmeal Cookies

Zaleti *Makes about 5 dozen*

⅔ cup (100 g) seedless raisins
½ cup (120 ml) grappa
3 cups (400 g) finely ground yellow cornmeal
2 cups (250 g) all-purpose flour
1 cup (200 g) sugar
2 teaspoons (8 g) baking powder
10 tablespoons (1¼ sticks) (180 g) unsalted butter, at room
　　temperature
1 cup (240 ml) milk
2 large eggs
1 teaspoon (4 g) pure vanilla extract
Grated zest of 1 lemon
½ cup (60 g) pine nuts
Confectioners' sugar for dusting

Place the raisins in a small bowl and cover with the grappa and ½ cup warm water. Set aside for at least an hour to plump the raisins.

Preheat the oven to 350°F. Line two baking sheets with parchment paper.

In a large bowl, combine the cornmeal, flour, sugar, and baking powder. Add pieces of the softened butter to the cornmeal mixture and begin stirring, or mixing with your hands, to incorporate. Or put the dry ingredients in the work bowl of a food processor fitted with a metal blade. Add the pieces of butter, and pulse five to six times until finely mixed. Transfer to a bowl.

In a small bowl, beat together the milk, eggs, and vanilla. Stir in the lemon zest.

Drain the raisins. Gradually add the milk mixture, raisins, and pine nuts to the dry ingredients, mixing until you have a soft dough.

Roll the dough into small ovals and place them on the prepared baking sheets about 2 inches apart. Lightly press down with your fingers to flatten. Bake until golden, about 15 minutes. Cool for 2 minutes on the sheet before using a spatula to transfer to a rack to cool. Store in an airtight container for up to 2 weeks. Dust with confectioners' sugar before serving.

Formaggi
The Cheese Course

WHILE CHEESE ISN'T AS COMMON on the traditional Venetian table as elsewhere in Italy, the Veneto produces some unique artisanal *formaggi*. At the end of the meal, we often indulge in an assortment of them, accompanied by sweet and spicy *mostarda,* a preserve that we make with kiwi from our country garden, and a glass of dessert wine.

We serve Asiago in its aged form *(stagionato),* when the flavor of this mild cow's milk cheese becomes more pronounced. Vezzeno, which is made near Asiago, has a more herbaceous, floral taste, since it's made with the milk of cows who graze on the mountainsides' wild flowers and grasses. Morlacco, a fresh cow's milk curd, is saltier and more pungent. Montasio, a rich, semisoft cow's milk cheese from Friuli, is also made in the Veneto. One of the stars of our cheese offering is Carnia from Friuli; it has a robust taste and is a bit sharper than Montasio but is aged for no more than two years.

Our cheese plate changes with the seasons and often includes fine cheese produced in other parts of Italy. Gorgonzola, the blue cow's milk cheese from Lombardia, is ideal *piccante,* when it's crumbly and slightly spicy. Formaggio di Fossa, a cow's milk cheese buried in leaves to age underground across Piemonte and Emilia-Romagna is earthy and delicious. To balance the offering, we serve caprino, or fresh goat's milk cheese. We recently introduced a truffled Toma, a mild semisoft cheese made with a mix of milks from the valleys of Piemonte and fragranced with white truffles.

Whether we're grating it over pasta, stirring it into risotto, or enjoying it on its own at the end of a meal, Parmigiano-Reggiano, the traditional aged cow's milk cheese produced in the areas around Parma and Reggio Emilia, is an essential ingredient in our kitchen. Home cooks may choose Grana, a less expensive aged cow's milk cheese for grating that's made outside the official Parmigiano-Reggiano designation, but at da Fiore, there's no substitute for the real thing.

The Wines of the Veneto

WHETHER THE OCCASION CALLS FOR A THIRTY–YEAR–OLD AMARONE IN A CRYSTAL REIDEL GOBLET AT DA FIORE, OR A YOUNG, RUSTIC Raboso tapped out of a barrel and into an ombra at the corner bar, there's a local wine to complement every aspect of our Venetian cuisine. Don't mistake our appreciation for overindulgence: As we say in Venice, *"Chi Dio ghe tolga l'acqua di no ghe piase vin"*—God will take water away from he who doesn't drink wine.

The Veneto is Italy's most productive wine-growing region, having recently surpassed Puglia and Sicily to claim the title. In part, our viticultural success stems from agreeable climatic conditions, but it's also in our blood. Wine production dates back to the ancient Etruscans here and flourished during the Roman Empire and Venetian Republic. Italy's oldest wine school, founded in 1876, continues today in Conegliano, the famed Prosecco region north of Treviso.

Wine-drinkers all over the world recognize our three most abundant varietals—the white Soave, and the red Bardolino and Valpolicella—because they were among the first Italian wines popularized in the United States. Servicemen stationed in the Veneto during World War II returned home with a taste for these light and fruity, easy drinking wines, and many large producers were more than happy to satisfy their demand with an abundant, inexpensive supply. The unfortunate consequence was overproduction and the sacrifice of sophisticated flavors and techniques that distinguished them in their native context. By the late seventies, local vintners were working hard to repair their image. Today, these wines have shaken the stigma and are enjoying international success yet again—this time with a much higher level of quality.

At da Fiore, many of our guests are surprised to find varieties that they recognize on our list of local wines. Merlot, Cabernet Sauvignon, and Sauvignon Blanc have grown here since the early part of the last century, when our region was ravaged by *Phylloxera*. As local vines were destroyed, farmers planted sturdier ones from France and the United States—and so these grapes became familiar here.

When reading wine labels from the Veneto, a few terms are helpful to know. Classico signifies that the grapes were grown and the wine was bottled in the original, traditional growing area and may be the product of old vines. Superiore usually refers to higher alcohol content and longer aging, which suggests a drier, more concentrated flavor. Wines that are labeled Frizzante have a subtle fizz, while Spumante refers to full-on bubbly. Tranquilo, as the word suggests, is a still wine.

The most unique term, and the most specific to the Veneto, is Recioto, which means that the grapes have been slightly dried to concentrate flavor. The name likely comes from *orecchio* or, in local dialect, *rècie,* which refers to the "ears" of the vine: crinkly, raisiny grapes that come from the outer part of the grape clusters. Since they have been fully exposed to the sun, more of the natural juice has turned to sugar on the vine. These grapes are usually dried longer, either in the sun or hung from rafters, to further intensify the flavor before they're finally fermented. The result can be either a dry Recioto (in which all of those concentrated sugars turn into alcohol) such as Amarone della Valpolicella, or a sweet dessert wine, if the fermentation is stopped when there's still enough sugar left.

Da Fiore's original wine list was small and select, with a house Prosecco and a Cabernet from Conegliano, and a few reliable, local bottles that Mara and Maurizio sought out on their day trips to small vineyards. As a bacaro, simplicity suited us fine. Over the years, as Mara's cooking called for more interesting wine pairings, our list expanded, and we took over a small cantina (above ground, as there are no cellars in Venice) around the corner from the restaurant. Our list grew to pay homage to nearby Alto Adige and Friuli as well, where we discovered aromatic strains such as Gewürztraminer, Tocai, and Reisling.

Our growing wine list mirrored a general rise in wine consciousness under way not just across Italy, but all over Europe and the United States. We soon realized that our Lista dei Vini couldn't ignore the great wines from other regions of Italy or France—Sancerre and Chablis, for example, were natural complements to our menu.

Today, wine is a more subjective study than ever before, and our wine list has come to reflect that. Though big reds upstage the delicate flavors of many of our dishes, they're cause for celebration on their own, and so there's a coveted place in our cantina for Barbera, Barolo, and even fine Bordeaux.

Veneto DOC and DOCG

For as long as Venetians have been drinking wine, there have been rules and regulations surrounding its production. It wasn't until the 1960s, however, that the government set forth official guidelines for geographic regions that produce traditional wines across Italy. DOC (Denominazione d'Origine Controllata) was formally implemented to assure consumers of a wine's origin, as well as its grape varieties and production requirements. At the time of writing, the Veneto alone has twenty-two DOCs, but the number is sure to climb as more local *consorzi* (groups of producers) lobby for recognition. In 1985, a *garantita,* or guarantee was added to some exclusive regions. Only three wines currently enjoy this DOCG status: Recioto di Soave, Bardolino Superiore, and Soave Superiore.

When a geographical region is granted DOC status, every wine that is made according to guidelines, regardless of quality, is DOC. Some artisanal producers are making superb wines that don't fit into these classifications, and we stock many of those wines in our cantina.

Here is a sampling of the Veneto's most recognizable DOC:

SOAVE DOC Named for the town where it's produced just east of Verona, this white is indeed suave, and its crisp character shines alongside a fish-dominant Venetian menu. Some producers have enhanced the classic Garganega-Trebbiano mix (both very light, local grapes) with some Chardonnay or Pinot Blanc.

Soave is made into a spumante, but it's the exquisite Recioto di Soave that we adore at da Fiore. The honeyed flavor of this dessert wine pairs beautifully with cheese.

BARDOLINO DOC This light and fruity ruby red wine is made just west of Verona, on the way to Lake Garda. With zippy hints of spice, it's an everyday wine that we think is best served cold. The region produces a rosato called Chiaretto that's dark pink, bone dry, and delicious with fish.

VALPOLICELLA DOC Aptly named "the valley of many cellars," Valpolicella is just north of Verona. A mix of the same grapes as Bardolino, but in different proportions, forms the basis for the fuller-bodied Valpolicella. The flavor is tart and light, with cherry overtones, and it pairs beautifully with fish.

Amarone, officially named Recioto della Valpolicella Amarone, is perhaps the Veneto's most revered wine, and certainly its most robust. Before the Valpolicella-mix grapes are crushed and fermented, the clusters are hung up to dry for as few as one or as many as three months, which further concentrates the sugars, which will turn to alcohol. At least a year's aging in oak casks imparts round woody flavors and smooths out the heavy tannins. It's these tannins that give Amarone its name—the word itself means "big tartness."

Amarone is one of Maurizio's favorite wines, which he reserves for the heartier, meatier meals in the country—it's extraordinary with lamb. As much as we adore it, Amarone tends to overpower the delicate nature of our fish dishes. The one exception is eel. We often suggest ordering Amarone, drinking a glass or two with your eel, and saving the rest for a plate of piquant cheese.

Amarone is a very dry, alcoholic wine, hovering between 13 and 18 percent, but its concentrated flavor suggests a subtle sweetness. It ages beautifully; and one of the most cherished bottles in our cantina is an Amarone bottled in 1922.

Also from the region, Recioto della Valpolicella (without the "Amarone") is a sweet dessert wine that's lovely with cheese and chocolate. *Ripasso,* which you won't find mentioned on all the labels that employ this method, refers to yet another technique. The skins and stems used in making Amarore are added to a regular Valpolicella, setting off a second round of fermentation. After some aging in wood casks, the result is rich and toasty, with deepened flavors and tannins, somewhere between a fruity Valpolicella and bold Amarone.

PROSECCO DOC Venetians adore Prosecco, sparkling or still, sweet or dry. The finesse of the slightly fizzy *frizzante* cleanses the palate and is a perfect foil for fish.

Prosecco comes from the region north of Treviso, where the Piave River cuts between Conegliano and Valdobbiadene. Just northeast of Valdobbiadene, in the township of Cartizze, is Prosecco's hilly Classico region, where some believe the best bottles are born. We've always served a "house" Prosecco at da Fiore. Ours is lightly sparkling, an almost twinkling version produced in Conegliano by one of the few vintners who still employs the traditional technique. Derived from the French *methode champanoise,* where fermentation occurs in the bottle instead of in modern stainless steel tanks, this old technique balances a natural acidity with a yeasty warmth. The yeast settles to the bottom of the bottle, so the wine must be decanted carefully, as not to mix the yeast back in. At da Fiore we pour it into traditional glass pitchers before pouring it into glasses.

Of the Veneto's remaining DOC wines, a few have grown in popularity outside of Italy in recent years. Bianco di Custoza, a dry, refreshing white wine blended with aromatic grapes such as Reisling and Tocai, pairs beautifully with fish. Colli Berici, the hilly region around Vicenza, is better known for reds: they blend local varietals such as Garganega with Cabernet Sauvignon and Merlot. Breganze, located north of Vicenza, bottles Cabernet, Merlot, Sauvignon Blanc, and others. Pinot Bianco, Cabernet, Chardonnay, and native grapes such as Moscato and Tocai flourish in the volcanic soil of the Colli Euganei, the hills that rise up from the Po Valley, near Padova. Producers make still and spumante wines with the Durello grape from the valley between Verona and Vicenza. Besides its supposed curative powers, the light, slightly acidic Lessini Durello white wine goes rather well with fish—particularly cod, which has long eluded wine experts looking for the perfect wine pairing.

Grappa

AT DA FIORE, dinner isn't over until Maurizio serves a glass of grappa. Grappa is a flavorful reincarnation of what wine leaves behind in its production. The tradition began in the fourteenth century, when wine was first distilled into a vapor, and reconstituted to concentrate its flavor. In the Veneto, the technique was applied to wine-making by-products, or pomace, as a resourceful attempt to coax out whatever little flavor remained.

Grappa producers used to travel from vineyard to vineyard after the grapes were crushed to distill the leftovers for families. The result was often harsh—a fortifier used more for medicinal purposes rather than sipped for enjoyment. A shot of it in the evening with an espresso *(caffè corretto)* could warm you for hours.

Grappa still runs the gamut in quality, from the commercially produced *supermercato* variety to those hand-wrought by experts who oversee every step of the distillation process. Producers also started experimenting with single varieties, which resulted in a more refined taste. Whether it's Marzemino, Soave, or even the rare Friulian Picolit, the distillation illustrates the grapes' core qualities. Especially when working with aromatic grapes like Moscato, the process requires acute attention in order to stop the distillation at just the right moment—keep it in the still too long and the flavor is lost. In order to allow for such careful observation, producers are working with much smaller quantities.

Grappa isn't just clear anymore. Aging in wood barrels imparts not just color but a depth and woodsy warmth of flavor that's reminiscent of a fine scotch. Other grappas are steeped with fruit, or made with different fruit juices, such as mirtillo (mulberries), cherries, and pears. At da Fiore, we often recommend fruit varieties as a first step toward appreciating grappa.

We appreciate the ceremony that surrounds the final note to a good meal and add to it with crystal grappa glasses, which have globe bottoms for swirling, and a tight mouth for concentrating the aroma. Grappas made with aromatic grapes such as Moscato call for a wider-rimmed glass to oxygenate and reveal their floral bouquet.

Bibliography

Agostini, Pino, and Alvise Zorzi. *A Tavola con I dogi.* Venezia: 1991.

Anderson, Burton. *Vino: The Wines and Winemakers of Italy.* Boston: Little, Brown, 1980.

Buonassisi, Vicenzo, and Luigi Carnacina. *Il Libro del Polenta.* Aldo Martello-Giunti Editore, 1974.

Contini, Mila. *Veneto in Boca.* Gulliver Edizione, n.p., n.d.

Conway, Linda Glick. *The Culinary Institute of America: The New Professional Chef.* 5th edition. New York: Van Nostrand Reinhold, 1991.

Da Mosto, Ranieri. *Il Veneto in Cucina.* Firenza: Giunti, 1974.

Davidson, Alan. *The Oxford Companion to Food.* New York: Oxford University Press, 1999.

Ghirardini, Gianni. *Cento Antiche Ricette di Cucina Veneziana.* Venezia: Alfieri, 1970.

Giordani Soika, Antonio. *La Laguna: Ambiemente Fauna e Flora.* Venezia: Corboi e Fiore Editori, 1992.

Goy, Richard J. *Chioggia and the Villages of the Venetian Lagoon: Studies in Urban History.* Cambridge: Cambridge University Press, 1985.

Grigson, Jane. *Fish Cookery.* London: Penguin Books, 1975.

Hazan, Marcella. *Marcella Cucina.* New York: HarperCollins, 1997.

Kurlansky, Mark. *Salt*. New York: Walker and Company, 2002.

Maffioli, Giuseppe. *Il Ghiottone Veneto*. Milano: Bramante Editrice, 1968.

———. *Cucina e vini delle tre Venezie*. Milano: U. Mursia, 1972.

———. *La Cucina Veneziana*. Padova: Franco Muzzio, ed., 1982.

McClane, A. J. *The Encyclopedia of Fish Cookery*. New York: Holt, Rinehart, and Winston, 1977.

Mintz, Sidney. *Sweetness and Power: The Place of Sugar in Modern History*. New York, 1985.

Morganti, Paolo. *Prodotti Veneti in Cucina*. Verona: Morganti, 2001.

Root, Waverly. *Foods of the World: The Cooking of Italy*. New York: Time Life Books, 1968.

———. *The Food of Italy*. New York: Vintage Books, 1971.

Salvatore de Zuliani, Mariu. *A tola co I nostri veci: La Cucina Veneziana*. Milano: F. Angeli, 1971.

Slow Food's *Italian Cheese*. Bra: Slow Food Arcigola Editore, 1999–2000.

Spector, Sally. *Venice and Food*. Verona: Arsenale Editrice, 1998.

Toso, Claudia. *The Cuisine of Doges, Columbines and Gondoliers in Venice*. Venice: Demetra, 1998.

Veronelli, Luigi. *The Food of Venice: Authentic Recipes from the City of Romance*. Singapore: Periplus, 2000.

Wright, Clifford. *A Mediterranean Feast*. New York: Morrow, 1999.

Zorzi, Elio. *Osterie Veneziane*. Venezia: Filippi Editore, 1967.

Index

strawberry grape sorbet, 199
sweet carnival fritters, 219–20
sweet focaccia with figs, 217
tiramisù Venetian style, 207
Turkish-style espresso sorbet, 198
Venetian bussolai, 228
Venetian fried cream, 215–16
warm chocolate cake da Fiore, 209–10
whipped pastry cream, 189
zabaione, 190

E

espresso sorbet, Turkish-style, 198

F

fennel, squid stuffed with imperial shrimp and,
    170–71
figs:
    fresh, red mullet stars with mint and,
      155
    sweet focaccia with, 217
filetto di San Pietro al pompelmo rosa, 143–44
fish:
    broth, 14
    buying of, 9–10
    cleaning and scaling of, 10
    cooking of, 11
    filleting of, 10–11
    frozen, 10
    storing of, 10
    see also specific fish
focaccia, sweet, with figs, 217
focaccia di fichi, 217

formaggi, 231
fritters, sweet carnival, 219–20
fritto di verdure di stagione, 57–59
frittura di moleche con insalata d'arance rucola,
    167–69
fruit:
    –filled polenta cake, 203–5
    soup, 195
fusilli con calamari e piselli, 85–86
fusilli with squid and peas, 85–86

G

galani, 221–22
ga'lani, 221–22
gamberetti (small shrimp), 124
garlic, 50
gelato, vanilla, pears poached in Veneto Merlot with,
    191–93
gelato di crema con pere cotte al vino rosso,
    191–93
gnocchi, pumpkin, with Parmigiano, sage, and white
    truffles, 91–93
gnocchi di zucca con Parmigiano, salvia, e tartufo,
    91–93
granseola con salsa di corallo, 51–53
grapefruit:
    pink, fillet of John Dory with, 143–44
    salad, sardines in fried bread with, 181–83
grape(s), strawberry:
    sorbet, 199
    spaghettini with imperial shrimp and, 79
Grappa, 237
grappini alle nocciole, 226
gratinata di scampi con carciofi e scamorza, 149–50
gratin of tagliolini with radicchio and shrimp,
    67–68

grouper, guanciale-wrapped, with broccoli and thyme
    soufflé, 162–63

H

halibut, in Venetian seafood stew, 115–17
hazelnut cookies, 226
herbs, aromatic:
    jumbo shrimp in bread "shirt" with, 157
    marinated striped bass with, 33
    risotto with, 105–7

I

insalate di arance e bianchetti scottati, 41
involtini di sarde con capperi e limone, 49–50
involtini di sogliola con zucchini, 176

J

John Dory, fillet of, with pink grapefruit, 143–44
juice, citrus, 12

L

lard, crostini with scampi in rosemary and, 35–36
le frittelle di carnevale, 219–20
lemon:
    rolled sardines with capers and, 49–50
    sorbet, with grated licorice, 197
licorice, grated, lemon sorbet with, 197
lobster, trenette with, 83–84

M

mazzancolle (imperial shrimp), 124
meringhe con le mandorle, 225
meringues with sliced almonds, 225
Merlot, Veneto, pears poached in, with vanilla gelato,
    191–93
mint:
    chilled soup, with sautéed oysters, 126–27
    red mullet stars with fresh figs and, 155
misto crudo di pesce alla Mediterranea, 27–79
monkfish:
    in fish broth, 14
    Mediterranean-style fillets, 145–47
    in Venetian seafood stew, 115–17
mousse, chestnut, with persimmon sauce,
    212–13
mousse di castagne, 212–13
mullet, red, 152
    in fish broth, 14
    in Mediterranean-style ceviche, 27–29
    ragù, spaghetti with cornetti, fresh tomatoes and,
        81–82
    rolled, with radicchio and spinach, 151–52
    sautéed baby, with blood orange segments,
        41
    stars, with fresh figs and mint, 155
    in Venetian seafood stew, 115–17
mushrooms, *see* porcini
mussels:
    da Fiore steamed, 39
    in Venetian seafood stew, 115–17

N

nettle, wild, and imperial shrimp soup, 121–23

Prosecco DOC, 236
pumpkin gnocchi with Parmigiano, sage, and white
truffles, 91–93
puntarelle salad, warm striped bass with, 31–32

R

radicchio, 69
di Treviso, marinated, 56
gratin of tagliolini with shrimp and, 67–68
rolled red mullet with radicchio and, 151–52
radicchio di Treviso marinato, 56
ragù, red mullet, spaghetti with cornetti, fresh
tomatoes and, 81–82
raisins, apple crown with cinnamon pastry cream and,
201–2
ratafia' sorbetto di caffè, 198
ravioli, seafood, with seasonal vegetable sauces, 95–97
ravioli di pesce con sugo di verdure di stagione, 95–97
red mullet, *see* mullet, red
rice:
da Fiore baked, 17
peas and, 113–14
see also risotto
risi e bisi, 113–14
riso al forno, 17
risotto, 98
with aromatic herbs, 105–7
butternut squash, drizzled with aged balsamic
vinegar, 109
rice and peas, 113–14
shrimp, with seasonal flavors, 103–4
Venetian black squid ink, 99
risotto con scampi e sapori di stagione, 103–4
risotto con seppie nero, 99
risotto di erbe aromatiche, 105–7
risotto di zucca e Parmigiano con aceto balsamico, 109
rolled fillet of sole with zucchini, 176

rolled red mullet with radicchio and spinach, 151–52
rolled sardines with capers and lemon, 49–50
rombo al forno in crosta di patate, 177–79
rosemary:
crostini with scampi in lard and, 35–36
sauce, 27
seared tuna slices with, 159–61
rotoli di triglia con radicchio di Treviso e spinaci, 151–52

S

saffron, pappardelle with oysters and, 71–72
sage, pumpkin gnocchi with Parmigiano, white
truffles and, 91–93
salads:
arugula and orange, fried soft-shell crabs on,
167–69
grapefruit, sardines in fried bread with, 181–83
puntarelle, warm striped bass with, 31–32
salsa, whole wheat pasta with, 89–90
saltata di cozze alla fiore, 39
salt crust, roasted sea bass in, 180
saor, see sweet and sour
saor di oratine alla Marco Polo, 43–44
sarde aperte impanate e fritte con insalatina con pompelmo,
181–83
sarde in saor, 45–47
sardines:
in fried bread with grapefruit salad, 181–83
rolled, with capers and lemon, 49–50
Venetian-style sweet and sour, 45–47
in whole wheat pasta with salsa, 89–90
sauces:
caper and thyme, 27
coral, spider crab with, 51–53
dill, 29
onion, 29
persimmon, chestnut mousse with, 212–13

About the Authors

DAMIANO MARTIN inherited his love of Venetian cuisine from his parents, da Fiore's proprietors Maurizio and Mara Martin. Since opening da Fiore in 1978, the Martins have nurtured their family restaurant from a popular trattoria serving sublime seafood into an international culinary destination that has been awarded a Michelin Star. After studying restaurant management in Berlin and working as a sommelier and manager in New York, Damiano returned to Venice as da Fiore's director in the late 1990s.

MARA MARTIN's extraordinary fishcentric cuisine has garnered a devout following in Venice and beyond. A self-taught cook, Mara's fresh approach to traditional Venetian cooking was a welcome stimulus to the restaurant scene in Venice during the early 1980s.

MAURIZIO MARTIN is da Fiore's congenial and charismatic host. When he is not chatting with guests and overseeing elegant evenings in the dining room, he is planning menus with Mara, sourcing ingredients from small-scale producers across the Veneto, and managing the cantina.

Da Fiore (*www.dafiore.com*) is located in the historic San Polo district, and is open for lunch and dinner from Tuesday through Sunday. Reservations can be made by calling +39 041 721 308, faxing +39 041 721 343, or e-mailing martin-damiano@libero.it. Da Fiore closes for a week during Fermo Pesca, the period when fishing is prohibited in the Venetian lagoon.

DANA BOWEN is a freelance food and travel writer who divides her time between New York City and upstate New York.